CLINICAL TRIAL MANAGEMENT

Edited by

Dr Shiva Murthy N
MBBS, MD, MBA

Dr Basavanna PL
MBBS, MD

Dr Chinmaya Mahapatra
M. Pharm, PhD

Dr Sanjeev Gupta
MBBS (MD Moscow), MD

Features
- Multiple Experienced at Director/Consultant/Senior professor/academician level Authors
- All articles written by speakers/participants of MPS NCTS-2023 Conference
- Program was well appreciated by the participants
- Widely circulated
- Available in JPADR Journal website

Main Sponsor	Associate Sponsor	In association with Dept. of Pharmacology	In association with JPADR Journal
Clini Med LIFESCIENCES PRIVATE LIMITED	**ETHIXINN** Your Research Companion	**CDSIMER** Dr. Chandramma Dayananda Sagar Institute of Medical Education and Research	JPADR

Dedicated to
all the colleagues
in the Clinical Research Industry

- By **MPS NCTS 2023 team**

Book Title: "CLINICAL TRIAL MANAGEMENT"
Published by Medical Pharmacologists Society

©**Copyrights 2023,** Medical Pharamcologists Society, Bangalore, Karnataka and Authors of respective articles **(speakers of MPS NCTS 2023 Conference)**

Managing Editor: Dr Shiva Murthy N
Other editorial board members: Dr Basavanna PL, Dr Chinmaya Mahapatra, and Dr Sanjeev Gupta.

Address for communication/Office address:
Dr Shiva Murthy N, SowmyaShiva Sadana, No 57, 1st cross, 4th main,
Kothanur Dinne, JP Nagar 8th Phase, Bangalore – 560078, Karnataka, India
Phone: +91 8884328275
Email: mps.mdpharmacologists@gmail.com
We do not have any other office.
For sales, please write to mps.mdpharmacologists@gmail.com

Website: www.mps.mdpharmac.org

First Edition: August 2023

Paper Size: A4

No of Pages: 135 pages including cover pages

Cost: Price: Hard bound copy—10 USD (Ten USD)

Note: The funds generated will be used for launching and maintenance of **Journal of Medical Pharmacologists Society (JMPS).**

Original soft copy designed and prepared and maintained by: **Dr. Shiva Murthy N, Founder President, Medical Pharmacologists Society**

KDP ISBN: 9798861512572
9798861512572

Table of Contents

Table of Contents contd.

Message from President, Medical Pharmacologists Society

I am happy to note that the Medical Pharmacologists Society is organising the National Clinical Trial Summit from August 5–6, 2023, in collaboration with CDSIMER and JPADR after obtaining sponsorship from ClinicMed Life Sciences (the main sponsor) and Ethixinn CRS (the associate sponsor).

Clinical Trials are the fastest way to develop new therapeutic agents. The data generated from clinical trials should be authentic and verified. Good Clinical Practice Guidelines provide guidelines to ensure clinical trials are planned properly and the data generated is verified for its quality. GCP also provides public assurance by helping us conduct audits and establish the audit trail of data generated for its reproducibility. Therefore, it is important for all investigators and their team members to undergo training in GCP.

I am happy to inform you that the MPS NCTS 2023 programme team has done an excellent job in preparing the comprehensive agenda, which is meticulously drafted. We can also find that highly experienced clinical research professionals, statisticians, ethics committee members, and pharma industry friends joined together to make this MPS NCTS 2023 programme a master piece. I hope the participants will get the benefit of learning from leaders, which further helps them perform well as clinical research investigators in their current or upcoming roles.

In addition to the above, I am happy to mention that all the learned speakers came forward to contribute a chapter to this e-book. I thank everyone, as an organising secretary/president of MPS, for their excellent contribution as a speaker and author of a chapter in this book. I am sure this will remain a good memory for years to come and will leave a mark as a significant milestone in the history of MPS achievements and in each and every speaker's or contributor's mind too.

I am glad to present to you this e-book, which is a compilation of the 22 articles on Clinical Trial Management.

Dr. Shiva Murthy N
President MPS and
Organising secretary, MPS NCTS 2023

Message from Organizing Chairman of MPS NCTS 2023 conference

The Medical Pharmacologists Society (MPS) is continuously trying to organise good programmes for the benefit of MD pharmacologists and also for increasing the skills of professionals and academicians working in the health care and clinical research industries. The MPS National Clinical Trial Summit (MPS NCTS 2023) is scheduled for August 5–6, 2023. We thank the organisations that helped us conduct this programme. CDSIMER Medical College and JPADR Journal added great strength to MPS NCTS 2023 programme through their untiring support. The sponsors of this programme, such as CliniMed Life Sciences (the main sponsor) and Ethixinn CRS (the associate sponsor), further fueled this programme to take it to the next level.

Training programmes like MPS NCTS 2023 will go a long way in strengthening the clinical researchers of this country, and similar programmes should be conducted more often. Training programmes like this help to reinforce the importance of GCP and the proper conduct of clinical trials as per ethical standards. This will enhance the confidence of the international community in the acceptability of the data generated from India.

I am happy to inform you that the MPS NCTS 2023 programme was well received, and we thank all the speakers and participants for extending support to this programme.

In addition to the above, I also thank all the speakers who came forward to contribute a chapter to this e-book. I thank everyone, as an organising chairman/member of the board of MPS, for their excellent contribution as a speaker and author of a chapter in this book. I am sure this will remain a good memory for years to come and will leave a mark as a significant milestone in the history of MPS achievements and in each and every speaker's or contributor's mind too.

I am glad to present to you this e-book, which is a compilation of the 22 articles on Clinical Trial Management.

Dr Basavanna PL
Organizing Chairman MPS NCTS 2023
Board member, MPS

Acknowledgement

Thanks to all the office bearers and life members of Medical Pharmacologists Society for whole hearted support extended till date to all the activities conducted by MPS.

Thanks to all the registered participants and all the members from Worldwide CR Leaders, Sites and SMOs network, Global herbal drug industry professional network groups.

We also thank all the MD Pharmacologists groups at national and state level for supporting MPS NCTS 2023 program.

Thanks to Sponsors, Supporting organization, Speakers, Authors and Organizing committee members.

Organizing Chairman
Dr. Basavanna PL

Organizing Secretary
Dr. Shiva Murthy N

Moderators
Day one — Dr. Chinmaya Mahapatra
Day two — Dr. Sanjeev Gupta

Organizing team
Mr. Dara Sai Ravi Teja
Dr. Siva Sankar Parasa

Prestigious Panel of Speakers

Dr. Shambo S Samajdar
Dr. Somanath Basu
Dr. Suyog Sindhu
Mr. Anirudh Sahoo
Dr. Gayathri Vishwakarma

Dr. Sapna Patil
Mrs. Vaishali Deshpande
Dr. Anuradha HV
Mr. Snehendu Koner

Dr. Meeta Amit Burande
Mrs. Renuka Neogi
Dr. Prajakt Barde
Dr. Akash Gadgade

Dr. Abhijit Munshi
Mrs. Lakshmi Achuta
Ms. Karishma Rampilla
Mr. Manish Singh Yadav

Chapter 01

An overview of drug development

Dr Ravi D Mala[1] and Dr Shiva Murthy N[2]

[1]Dr Ravi D Mala, MBBS, MD

Associate Professor, Dept of Pharmacology, Dr Chandramma Dayananda Sagar Institute of Medical Education and Research (CDSIMER), Dayananda Sagar University, Ramanagara, Karnataka.

[2] Dr Shiva Murthy N, MBBS, MD, MBA

President, Medical Pharmacologists Society (MPS), and Professor, Dept of Pharmacology, Dr Chandramma Dayananda Sagar Institute of Medical Education and Research (CDSIMER), Dayananda Sagar University, Ramanagara, Karnataka.

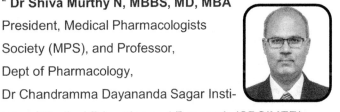

Abstract

New drug development is a continuous requirement. New drugs are developed to treat new diseases, address the limitations of existing drugs like their inefficiency in newly identified diseases, high toxicity with a low desired response, an inconvenient route of administration leading to lower patient compliance or more chances of drug interactions, and also have contraindications in special populations. New drugs can be identified by identifying newer targets and developing newer analogues, derivatives, or substitutes for the existing drugs. The new drug must be a better alternative against a clinical condition or disease, have maximum efficacy and minimal acceptable adverse effects, and have better patient compliance. Clinical trials are the fastest way to develop drugs and make them available for clinical use. The objective of this article is to give an overview of the drug development process.

Introduction:

Why do we need a new drug?

As a Pharmacologists we know that there are a number of drugs with different mechanisms of action, doses, and dosage forms available on the market to treat a clinical condition or disease. To overcome the limitations of existing drugs, like their inefficiency in newly identified diseases, high toxicity with low desired response, inconvenient route of administration leading to less patient compliance, more chances of drug interactions, and also having contraindications in special populations.

How do we address these limitations?

By the development of a new drug or the discovery of new analogues, derivatives, or substitutes from the existing drug. The new drug must be a better alternative against a clinical condition or disease, have maximum efficacy and minimal acceptable adverse effects, and have better patient compliance.

As it is a costly affair to develop a new drug because it takes a minimum of 12–15 years, that's roughly 1/3 of the duration of the entire professional career for any of us, and it needs to invest nearly $1 Billion, which is equivalent to employing 665+ employees at an annual salary of $100k for 15 years. In Indian currency, it accounts for nearly 7 to 8 thousand crore rupees.

Corresponding author: **Dr Shiva Murthy N** Can be contacted at phone number+91 8884328275.
Email id: shivuindia@gmail.com

A new drug can be developed by different methods, as follows;

- By Chemical Modification, e.g., Penicillin to ampicillin or amoxicillin
- Synthesis of analogues, Agonists, and Antagonists (e.g., PGs)
- Traditional medicines, e.g., Physostigmine to Neostigmine
- Structure Activity Relationship (SAR): e.g., fluroquinolones
- Prodrug form: e.g., L-Dopa to Dopamine
- Recombinant DNA technology (e.g., insulin, erythropoietin)
- Enantiomer: Dextro or Levo E.g., Esomeprazole: better oral bioavailability; Levofloxacin: slower excretion

What are the sources for the development of a new drug?

- Random Screening
- Serendipity: accidental discovery (Penicillin by Alexander Fleming)
- Toxic plants, poisons, and teratogens
- Metals and Salts
- Synthetic
- Recombinant DNA Technology
- Modification of the structure of existing drugs
- Search for a safer indication for a failed drug (Thalidomide)

How is a New Drug Developed? Discovery and Development

- Stages of drug discovery and development include
- Target identification and validation
- Lead identification and optimisation
- Product characterization and Formulation
- Preclinical research
- Investigational New Drug Application
- Clinical trials and New Drug applications
- Approval

The drug discovery process ends when one lead compound is found for a drug candidate, and the process of drug development starts.

Once a molecule is approved, it must be manufactured according to high standards of purity and stability as prescribed by regulations. Although manufacturing is not usually a concern for discovery biologists, the process of manufacturing a new medicine can be complex and expensive, particularly for biological products.

Preclinical Research

Once a lead compound is found, drug development begins with preclinical research to determine the efficacy and safety of the drug in experimental animals.

Researchers determine about the drug's:
- Pharmacokinetic information
- Potential benefits and mechanisms of action
- Best dosage, and suitable route of administration
- Side effects/adverse events
- Effects on gender, race, or ethnicity groups
- Interaction with other drugs
- Effectiveness compared to similar drugs

Preclinical trials, test the new drug on non-human subjects for its efficacy, toxicity, and pharmacokinetic (PK) information.

These trials are conducted in vitro and in vivo with an unrestricted dose.

Proof of Principle or Proof of Concept

Proof of Principle (PoP) studies are those that are successful in preclinical trials and early safety testing. Proof of Concept (PoC) terminology is used almost interchangeably with PoP in drug discovery and development projects.

Successful PoP and PoC studies lead to programme advancement to Phase II studies of drugs.

In Vivo, In Vitro, and Ex Vivo Assays:

These three types of studies are conducted on whole living organisms or cells, including animals and humans, or on dead tissue or its extract.
In-vivo preclinical research involves the development of new drugs using mouse, rat, and dog models.

In-vitro research is research conducted in a laboratory.

Ex-vivo uses cells or tissues from a sacrificed animal.

Examples of ex-vivo research assays are finding effective cancer treatment agents; measurements of tissue properties (physical, thermal, electrical, and optical); and realistic modelling for new surgical procedures. In an ex-vivo assay, a cell is always used as the basis for small explant cultures that provide a dynamic, controlled, and sterile environment.

In Silico Assays

In silico assays are test systems or biological experiments performed on a computer or via computer simulation. These are expected to become most popular with the ongoing improvements in computational power and behavioural understanding of molecular dynamics and cell biology.

Drug Delivery

A new drug can be delivered by oral, topical, membrane, intravenous, or inhalation. Drug delivery systems are used for targeted delivery or controlled release of new drugs. Physiological barriers in animal or human bodies may prevent drugs from reaching the targeted area or being released when needed. The goal is to prevent the drug from affecting healthy tissues while still being therapeutically effective.

Formulation Optimisation and Improving Bioavailability

Formulation optimisation is ongoing throughout the preclinical and clinical stages. It ensures drugs are delivered to the desired site at the right time and in the right concentration.

Clinical Development

Once preclinical research is complete, researchers move on to clinical drug development, including clinical trials and volunteer studies to fine-tune the drug for human use.

Investigational New Drug (IND) Application

IND applications are submitted to the FDA before starting clinical trials. If clinical trials are ready to be conducted and the FDA has responded positively about the drug, the concerned people may start the clinical trials.

Clinical Trials– Dose Escalation, Single Ascending, and Multiple Dose Studies

Proper dosing determines medication effectiveness, and clinical trials examine dose escalation, single ascending, and multiple dose studies to determine the best dose for the patients.

Phases 0 and I: Healthy Volunteer Study

First time the drug is tested on humans; less than 100 healthy volunteers are enrolled in Phase I of the clinical trial. This phase may be preceded by Phase-0, also called a microdosing study, where $1/100^{th}$ of the dose is administered to a few (10–12) healthy volunteers. This helps determine whether the drug reaches its target site. Phase-0 is optional for the manufacturers. But, still, many companies try to conduct Phase-0 studies to know their success rate in clinical trials and to proceed with the same.

Phase I is done to assess the safety and pharmacokinetic effects on the body, as well as any side effects, for a safe dose range.

Phase II and Phase III: Studies in the Patient Population

Phase II assesses drug safety and efficacy in an additional 100–500 patients, who may receive a placebo or a standard drug used before. Analysis of optimal dose strength helps create drug schedules while recording adverse events and risks.

Phase III enrols 1,000–5,000 patients, enabling medication labelling and instructions for the proper use of drugs. Phase III trials require extensive collaboration, organisation, and Independent Ethics Committee (IEC) or Institutional Review Board (IRB) coordination and regulation in anticipation of full-scale production following drug approval.

DCGI/FDA Review

Once the new drug has been formulated for its best efficacy and safety, and the results from clinical trials are available, it is advanced further for FDA review. Meanwhile, the FDA reviews and approves the new drug application submitted by the drug development company.

Regulatory Approval Timeline

The new drug regulatory approval timeline may be standard, fast track, breakthrough, accelerated approval, or priority review, depending on its applications and necessity for patients. If a standard or priority review is required, the approval timeline may be up to a year. Fast-track, breakthrough, or accelerated approvals may occur sooner.

NDA, ANDA, and BLA Applications

A new drug application (NDA), abbreviated new drug application (ANDA), or Biologics Licence Application (BLA) is submitted to the FDA after clinical trials demonstrate the safety and efficacy of the drug. The FDA reviews the study data and decides whether to grant approval or not. Additional research or an expert advisory panel may be required before a final decision is made.

Accelerated Approval

New drugs may be granted accelerated approval if there is strong evidence of a positive impact on a surrogate endpoint instead of evidence of an impact on the actual clinical benefits the drug provides. An expedition of approval means the medication can help treat severe or life-threatening conditions.

Reasons for Drug Failure

New drug applications may fail for a variety of reasons, including toxicity, efficacy, PH properties, bioavailability, or inadequate drug performance.

Post-market monitoring and surveillance

Following drug approval and manufacturing, the FDA directs drug companies to monitor the safety of their drugs using the FDA Adverse Event Reporting System (FAERS) database. FAERS helps the FDA implement its post-marketing safety surveillance programme. Through this programme, manufacturers, health professionals, and consumers report rare and chronic adverse effects of approved drugs.

Drug Master File

A Drug Master File (DMF) is a submission to the FDA used to provide confidential, detailed information about facilities, processes, or articles used in the manufacturing, processing, packaging, and storage of a human drug.

Conclusion :

New drug development is a highly regulated, complicated process that requires specialists and intense research and development skill sets in the medical research community. All regulations and safety indications must be observed carefully, and human and animal clinical trial subjects must be treated professionally and with the utmost care. The goal of drug development is to prevent human and animal pain and suffering whenever possible and to find and provide new drugs that we can depend on to improve our health and happiness.

References :

1. Tripathi, K. D. (2018). Essentials of medical pharmacology (8th ed.). Jaypee Brothers Medical.

2. Goodman & Gilman's: The Pharmacological Basis of Therapeutics, 13e Brunton LL, Hilal-Dandan R, Knollmann BC. Brunton L.L., & Hilal-Dandan R, & Knollmann B.C.(Eds.).Eds. Laurence L. Brunton, et al.

3. US Food and Drug Administration . US Department of Health and Human Services; Rockville, MD: 2015. Guidance for Industry. Estimating the Maximum Safe Starting Dose in Initial Clinical Trials for Therapeutics in Adult Healthy Volunteers.

4. Mohs RC, Greig NH. Drug discovery and development: Role of basic biological research. Alzheimers Dement (N Y). 2017 Nov 11;3 (4):651-657. doi: 10.1016/j.trci.2017.10.005. PMID: 29255791; PMCID: PMC5725284.

5. Akhondzadeh S. The Importance of Clinical Trials in Drug Development. Avicenna J Med Biotechnol. 2016 Oct-Dec;8(4):151. PMID: 27920881; PMCID: PMC5124250.

6. Spedding M. New directions for drug discovery. Dialogues Clin Neurosci. 2006;8(3):295-301. doi: 10.31887/DCNS.2006.8.3/mspedding. PMID: 17117611; PMCID: PMC3181825.

Chapter 02

Evolution and Principles of GCP

Dr Chinmaya Mahapatra[1] and Dr Shiva Murthy N[2]

[1]**Dr Chinmaya Mahapatra, M Pharm, PhD**
Associate Professor & HOD, TNU,
LQPPV (PvOI) IntuVigilance, UK,
Editor-in-Chief, JPADR Journal,
Founder President
Global Pharmacovigilance Society. Odisha.
.

[2] **Dr Shiva Murthy N, MBBS, MD, MBA**
President, Medical Pharmacologists
Society (MPS),
and Professor, Dept of Pharmacology,
Dr Chandramma Dayananda Sagar
Institute of Medical Education and Research (CDSIMER),
Dayananda Sagar University,

Abstract

Objectives: To provide brief information about the reasons behind the development of Good Clinical Practice guidelines and discuss briefly the basic principles of Good Clinical Practice keeping the ICH E6 guidelines as a reference. Good Clinical Practice (GCP) originated from the need for standardised guidelines and ethical principles to ensure the protection of human subjects participating in clinical trials. The development of GCP can be traced back to the aftermath of World War II and the Nuremberg trials, which exposed the unethical experiments conducted by Nazi physicians on human subjects. After this GCP guidelines document was finalised in 1996 and became effective in 1997, initially it was just a guideline for conducting clinical trials or research. Later, it was incorporated into various laws across the world. In this article, a detailed history of the evolution of GCP and 13 principles of GCP are discussed.

Introduction

Preclinical research helps us understand the drug's safety to some extent. But does not give a complete safety profile for human subjects. Clinical trials and research help us close this gap. We can assure the quality of the outcomes of clinical trials and research by following Good clinical practice guidelines. The objectives of the article are to provide brief information about the reasons behind the development of Good Clinical Practice guidelines and discuss briefly the basic principles of Good Clinical Practice keeping the ICH E6 guidelines as a reference.

Definition of Good clinical practice

Good Clinical Practice (GCP) is an international ethical and scientific quality standard for the design, conduct, performance, monitoring, auditing, recording, analysis, and reporting of clinical trials.

Corresponding author: Dr Shiva Murthy N. Can be contacted at phone number+91 8884328275
Email id: shivuindia@gmail.com

GCP provides assurance that the data and reported results are credible and accurate, and that the rights, integrity, and confidentiality of trial subjects are respected and protected.

History of the development of GCP

Good Clinical Practice (GCP) originated from the need for standardised guidelines and ethical principles to ensure the protection of human subjects participating in clinical trials. The development of GCP can be traced back to the aftermath of World War II and the Nuremberg trials, which exposed the unethical experiments conducted by Nazi physicians on human subjects.

In response to these atrocities, the World Medical Association (WMA) established the Declaration of Helsinki in 1964. The Declaration provided ethical principles for medical research involving human subjects and emphasised the need for informed consent, respect for individuals, and the importance of the benefits outweighing the risks.

Over time, as the field of clinical research grew and became more complex, there was a need for more comprehensive guidelines to ensure the integrity and reliability of clinical trial data. In 1989, the International Conference on Harmonisation of Technical Requirements for Registration of Pharmaceuticals for Human Use (ICH) was established as a global collaboration between regulatory authorities and the pharmaceutical industry. The ICH aimed to develop harmonised guidelines to facilitate the registration of pharmaceutical products worldwide.

One of the major achievements of the ICH was the development of the ICH E6 guideline, titled "Good Clinical Practice: Consolidated Guideline." This guideline, published in 1996, provided a standardised framework for the design, conduct, monitoring, and reporting of clinical trials. It incorporated ethical principles from the Declaration of Helsinki and addressed important aspects of trial conduct, such as subject protection, data integrity, and sponsor responsibilities.

The ICH E6 guideline has been adopted by regulatory authorities worldwide, and it serves as the basis for GCP regulations in many countries. It has been periodically updated to incorporate advancements in technology, data management, and risk-based approaches to trial monitoring.

Overall, the origin of Good Clinical Practice can be attributed to the need for ethical standards and guidelines to protect human subjects and ensure the reliability of clinical trial data. Its evolution has been driven by international collaborations and the recognition of the importance of global harmonisation in clinical research.

The history has been presented in the following figures sequentially, from Fig.1 to Fig 6. (self explanatory)

When these guidelines was were made effective?

GCP guidelines document was finalised in 1996 and became effective in 1997, but it was just a guideline for conducting clinical trials or research.

Figure No. 1

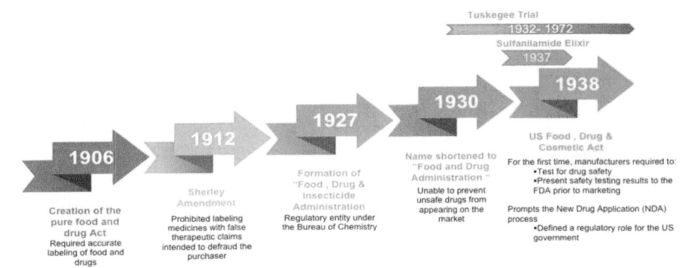

Figure No. 2

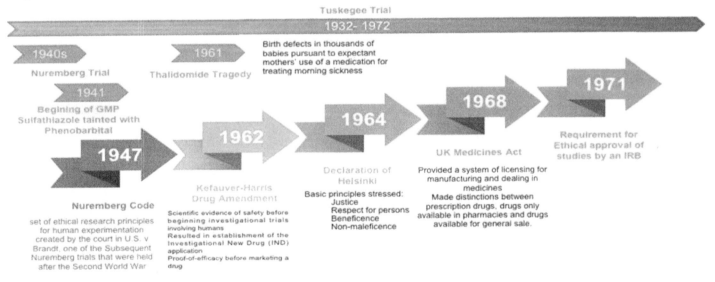

Figure No. 3

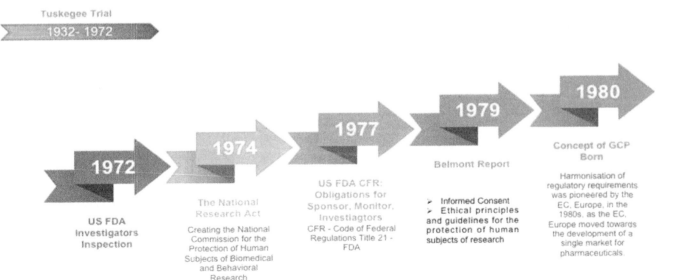

Figure No. 4

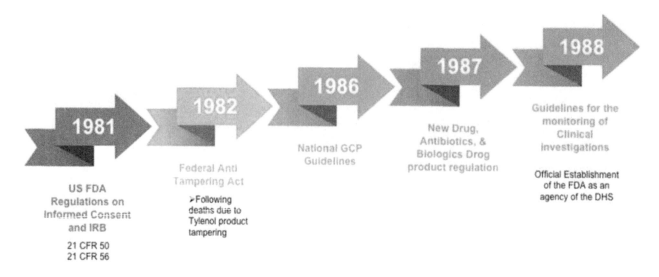

Figure No. 5

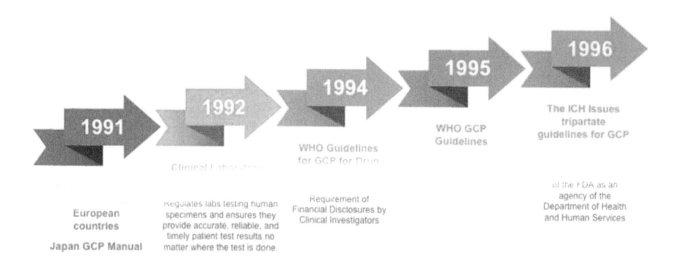

Figure No. 6

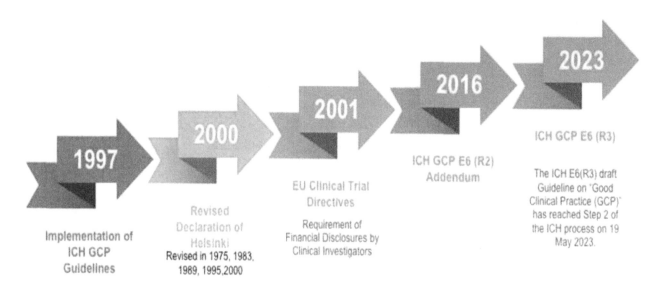

In 2004, the European Union (EU) introduced "The Medicines for Human Use (Clinical Trials) Regulations 2004 and the Directive on Good Clinical Practice. This changed the way the world looked at GCP, and it became a legal obligation in the UK/Europe for all trials involving the investigation of medicinal products.

Again in India, Indian GCP guidelines were released in 2001. But until 2005, it was not mandatory to follow, as it was not a legal requirement. Due to this reason, many investigators did not take steps to follow the guidelines. Then in 2005, CDSCO made major revisions to Schedule Y (which is part of the Drugs and Cosmetic Act 1940 (D and C Act) and Drugs and Cosmetic Rules of 1945) and upgraded Indian legal requirements with the objective of making it an internationally accepted definition and procedure.

After this, numerous amendments to India's clinical trial regulations were made between 2005 and 2015. In spite of all these, many loopholes remain in the legal requirements for conducting clinical trials in India.

In 2016, based on the Supreme Court of India (the apex court in India) and various committee recommendations, a series of amendments to the Drugs and Cosmetics Rules were issued by the Ministry of Health and Family Welfare with the objective of restoring faith in the Indian clinical trial industry. Finally, a draft of the New Drugs Clinical Trials Rules-2019 (NDCT 2019) was released by the central government in the Gazette of India under the aegis of the Drugs and Cosmetics Act of 1940 on March 19, 2019.

Again, in the NDCT 2019 rules, GCP continues to be the legal requirement while conducting clinical trials in India.

What are the basic principles of GCP?

The main objective of the GCP guidelines is to ensure that experimentation on humans is done for the purpose of advancement in medical sciences and serves as a quality benchmark as well as a moderator that keeps such experimentation under monitoring. It also defines the standard operational requirements of a clinical trial. In addition, it also defines the roles and responsibilities of the officials involved in conducting these trials. The latest GCP requirements are laid out in the document named ICH E6 (R2) Good Clinical practice.

Principles of GCP

Principle 1: Basic Ethical Principles Originating from the Declaration of Helsinki
Research that involves humans should be

- Scientifically sound
- Conducted in line with basic ethical principles originating from the Declaration of Helsinki.

The three important principles that permeate all other GCP principles are:

- Equal importance is associated with basic ethics while conducting CT.
- Recognition for persons involved in CT and principles of beneficence and justice.

This principle acknowledges the freedom and dignity of every participant. It requires obtaining informed consent from research subjects or their legally authorised representatives if the participant is a minor or not in the legal status to give valid consent.

This GCP principle also mandates that researchers maximise the benefits and minimise the harms associated with research for participants. Research should be conducted in such a way that research-related risks are reasonably reduced and participants are safeguarded from serious injuries.

This principle mandates equitable justice in the selection of subjects for trial by investigators. Also demands fair treatment of patients, irrespective of their consent to participate in the clinical trials. After enrolling in trials, GCP mandates proper treatment of subjects for their trial-related injuries.

Principle 2: Be Clear about Expected Risks and benefits.

Investigators should justify the benefits over the foreseeable risks and inconveniences to the participating subjects. Risks vs. Benefits ratio should be favourable and weighed against the anticipated benefit for the individual trial subject and society. Each trial should be initiated or continued only after justifying the benefits before the initiation of the trial and after initiation analysis at regular predefined intervals. Trial subjects should be discontinued or rescued if the risks are found to be greater.

during such intermittent analysis, and results are not expected to benefit that particular participating subject.

Principle 3: The Primary Trial Participant's Concerns

The rights, safety, and well-being of the trial subjects are the most important considerations and should prevail over the interests of science and society. If the trial is found to be beneficial to society but not to that particular subject, then that subject should be discontinued or rescued from trial-related risks.

Principle 4: Positive development experience with the investigational product

Information available based on previous basic investigations and preclinical and clinical investigations about the investigational product should justify adequately the plan to conduct future research activities with human participants. The available non-clinical and clinical information on an investigational product should be adequate to support the proposed clinical trial.

Principle 5: Scientifically sound protocol

Research should be conducted as per a protocol that is well written, detailed, scientifically sound, and approved by an ethics committee. If the protocol is amended for any reason, it should be brought to the attention of the ethics committee, and written approval should be documented before implementation of such a change.

The protocol's contents should be justified with valid data or evidence accrued to date.

Principle 6: Ethical clearance of clinical trial protocols, investigators, facilities, and procedures

All clinical trials should be initiated only after obtaining a favourable written opinion or approval by the institutional review board (IRB) or independent ethics committee (IEC). Such approvals should be issued by the ethics committee only after reviewing the protocol in an official IRB/IEC meeting.

The trial activities should be conducted only in compliance with the approved protocol.

Principle 7: Medical Decisions about Subjects or Participants Health

All medical decisions about the treatment of a participant's or patient's illness and the management of adverse drug reactions or health-related risks should be taken by an appropriately qualified medical or dental doctor. Therefore, it is most important to have an appropriately qualified doctor or physician as the principal investigator in the clinical trials. The doctor should be qualified by his or her education, training, and experience in managing such illnesses or clinical trials.

Principle 8: Qualified staff to conduct the clinical trial

All staff or team members who are given the task of managing any part of the clinical trial should be qualified by education, training, and experience to perform their respective tasks. Proper personal files should be maintained to demonstrate the qualifications of the staff. All the staff should be trained on standard operating procedures, and allotment of responsibilities should be done after completing such training and sufficient documentation of such training.

Principle 9: Freely given informed consent by participants

Freely given written consent should be documented by each participant before the initiation of any trial-related activity. Sufficient time should be given to participants to read and ask any questions that may need clarification. If the participant is a minor or does not have the cognitive ability to give consent, then an appropriate legal representative should give consent before going ahead with clinical trial-related procedures.

Principle 10: Clinical Trial Data

The quality of clinical trial data and reproducibility of the same for verification and auditing are most important. All clinical trial information should be recorded, handled, and stored in a way that allows for accurate reporting, interpretation, and verification. The data should be safeguarded from any form of destruction and maintained for the minimum number of years as per protocol or country regulations. Loss of data or failure to provide the data may disqualify the claims made about a trail or its results.

Principle 11: Confidentiality of Records

All personally identifiable information about the subjects should be kept confidential. The subject's privacy and dignity should be protected. The confidentiality rules, in accordance with the applicable regulatory requirement(s), should be adopted in the standard operating procedures and implemented.

Principle 12: Investigational Products

To ensure the authenticity, quality, efficacy, and safety of the investigational products (IP), they should be manufactured, handled, and stored in accordance with applicable Good Manufacturing Practice (GMP). The IP should be used (received, dispensed, distributed, dosed, reconciled, and destroyed) in accordance with the approved protocol.

Principle 13: Quality Assurance Systems

All clinical trial activities should be conducted as per established standard operating procedures. An independent monitor should verify the systems and procedures while conducting trial-related activities. All deviations should be recorded and reported to the sponsors and ethics committee. The same should be documented in the final report. Quality monitoring and assurance activities should be done during the pre-study, study, and post-study periods. The audit certificates should be filed in study reports.

All clinical trials should be conducted in compliance with the 13 principles of GCP.

Conclusion

Compliance with GCP will ensure the quality and acceptability of the data by regulatory agencies across the world. Every member of the clinical trial execution team should be trained on GCP and its principles. All team members should be aware of the historical aspects of the development of GCP and its evolution. This will help them realise the importance of GCP and its necessity.

Every clinical researcher should undergo GCP training at least once every two years to ensure reinforcement of the principles of GCP and to maintain awareness about GCP. All the clinical researchers should be made to attend the GCP training on a regular basis and be made aware of the consequences of non-compliance with the GCP guidelines and related fraudulent activities.

The Declaration of Helsinki and GCP will continue to remain the framework for ethical principles and guiding principles for the conduct of clinical trials and research and have become global laws to safeguard humanity as a whole.

References

1. ICH Harmonised Guideline Integrated Addendum to ICH E6(R1): Guideline For Good Clinical Practice [available in the website: https://database.ich.org/sites/default/files/E6_R2_Addendum.pdf] accessed on 9/Jul/2023

2. Indian GCP guidelines [available at https://cdsco.gov.in/opencms/opencms/system/modules/CDSCO.WEB/elements/download_file_division.jsp?num_id=MzM5NQ==] accessed on 9/Jul/2023

3. V. Vennu and p. P. Saini. India's Clinical Trial Regulatory Changes, Indian Researcher's Awareness of Recently Changed Regulations, and the Impact of the New Drugs and Clinical Trial Rules: A Review. Indian J Pharm Sci 2020;82(5):726-740

4. Mohammed Imran, Abul K. Najmi, Mohammad F. Rashid, Shams Tabrez, Mushtaq A. Shah. Clinical research regulation in India-history, development, initiatives, challenges and controversies: Still long way to go. J Pharm Bioall Sci 2013;5:2-9.

Chapter 03

Indian and International Regulations Governing Clinical Research

Shambo S Samajdar[1], Shreyashi Dasgupta[2], Sougata Sarkar[3]

[1]MBBS MD DM (Clinical Pharmacology), Diploma Allergy Asthma and Immunology (Gold Medal), PG Diploma Endo & Diabetes (RCP), Fellowship Respiratory & Critical Care (WBUHS); Consultant, Diabetes & Allergy-Asthma Therapeutics Specialty Clinic, Kolkata & Clinical Pharmacologist, Department of Clinical Pharmacology, STM Kolkata, West Bengal.

[2]MBBS MD DM (Clinical Pharmacology); Clinical Pharmacologist, Department of Clinical Pharmacology, STM Kolkata, West Bengal.

[3]MBBS MD DM (Clinical Pharmacology); Clinical Pharmacologist, Department of Clinical Pharmacology, STM Kolkata, West Bengal

Abstract

Introduction: The landscape of clinical research regulations in different regions, such as India, the United States (US), and the European Union (EU), plays a crucial role in shaping drug development, patient safety, and international collaboration. Understanding the similarities and differences in these regulatory frameworks is essential to promote effective and efficient clinical trials and ensure the highest standards of ethical conduct and patient protection. **Objective:** This systematic review aims to comprehensively analyze and compare the regulatory frameworks governing clinical trials in India, the United States (US), and the European Union (EU). By examining recent updates in Indian regulations and contrasting them with US and EU systems, this review assesses the potential impact on patient safety, drug development, and international collaboration. **Methods:** A systematic literature search was conducted to identify relevant studies and articles published up to 15-May-2023. Inclusion criteria encompassed publications discussing regulations pertaining to clinical research in India, the US, and the EU. Data were extracted and synthesized to compare key aspects of each regulatory system, focusing on patient protection, ethical standards, drug approval processes, and the promotion of medical advancements. **Results:** The findings reveal that India has implemented recent amendments to enhance ethical and quality standards for clinical trials, with a focus on attracting international trials and accelerating local drug development. The streamlined approval process for indigenous medicines aims to expedite clinical trial procedures. In contrast, the US and EU prioritize a balance between safety and efficacy while promoting medical advancements. The article outlines the divergent histories of drug and device regulation in these regions, leading to distinct regulatory differences. Nevertheless, collaborative efforts are underway to facilitate mutual standardization and openness in medical device approvals. **Conclusion:** This systematic review provides a comprehensive analysis of the regulatory landscapes governing clinical research in India, the US, and the EU. The recent updates in Indian regulations reflect an effort to strengthen patient safety and foster drug development, potentially attracting more international trials. The comparison with US and EU systems underscores the importance of collaboration among academic researchers, regulatory bodies, and the pharmaceutical industry in ensuring efficient and robust review processes while prioritizing patient protection and risk-benefit assessments.

Keywords: Clinical Research, Regulations, India, United States, European Union, Patient Safety, Drug Development.

Corresponding author: Dr Shambo S Samajdar. Can be contacted at phone number +91 98318 92425.
Email id: shambo_sa2001@yahoo.co.in

Introduction:

Clinical research is an indispensable aspect of modern medicine and plays a vital role in advancing healthcare practices, treatment modalities, and pharmaceutical innovations. At the heart of any medical institution, hospital, or university, academicians hold the responsibility of patient care, teaching, administration, and research. While these diverse roles offer immense satisfaction, it is research that remains the cornerstone for nurturing intellectual curiosity and driving evidence-based medicine.

The significance of sound research extends far beyond academic pursuit; it directly impacts patient outcomes and fosters better and more effective healthcare delivery, ultimately contributing to the overall promotion of health. However, the journey of research is riddled with challenges, as it demands significant time, labor, and resources, often stretching over months or even years to complete. Drug development research, in particular, is known for its complexity and length, with a single novel medication requiring an average investment of $1.78 billion and approximately 13.5 years to reach the market[1]. In the realm of drug development research, clinical trials, or regulatory studies, form the critical bridge between scientific discovery and real-world applications. These studies, encompassing Phase I to Phase IV trials, assess the safety, efficacy, and tolerability of investigational drugs and treatments. Academicians, primarily serving as principal investigators in academic centers, play a central role in conducting these trials. Often, the financial backing for such research emanates from the pharmaceutical industry, as they sponsor and ensure compliance with regulatory requirements. While industry-sponsored clinical trials are prevalent, academicians also embark on their independent research ventures, termed "Investigator Initiated Studies" (IISs). These studies are driven by the intellectual curiosity of researchers, who seek funding from diverse sources, which may include the pharmaceutical industry. In undertaking these IISs, academicians embrace dual roles as both investigators and sponsors, assuming direct accountability for adhering to regulatory standards throughout the research process[2].

As clinical research transcends geographical boundaries, understanding the nuances of Indian and international regulations governing this critical domain is paramount. These regulations serve as essential guidelines to ensure patient safety, ethical conduct, data integrity, and scientific rigor throughout the research journey. By delving into the intricacies of these regulations, we can gain invaluable insights into the ethical, legal, and operational aspects that underpin clinical research in both domestic and global contexts. In this exploration, we aim to shed light on the regulatory frameworks governing clinical research, thereby fostering a deeper understanding of its multifaceted impact on the medical landscape.

Methods:

A comprehensive research protocol was developed to guide the systematic review process. The research objectives were defined, focusing on the examination of Indian and international regulations governing clinical research. To identify relevant literature on clinical research regulations, a thorough search strategy was devised. Electronic databases, including PubMed, Embase, Scopus, Web of Science, and Google Scholar, were systematically searched. The search terms encompassed a combination of specific keywords and Medical Subject Headings (MeSH) terms related to clinical research regulations. The search terminology and MeSH terms used were: "Clinical research regulations", "Clinical trial regulations", "Ethical guidelines for clinical research", "Patient safety in clinical trials", "Informed consent in clinical research", "Data protection in clinical trials", "Oversight mechanisms in clinical research", "Indian clinical research regulations", "International clinical research regulations"

Indian National Regulatory Body:

In India, the Central Drugs Standard Control Organisation (CDSCO) serves as the National Regulatory Authority responsible for overseeing the safety, efficacy, and quality of pharmaceuticals, cosmetics, and medical devices. Operating under the Indian Ministry of Health and Family Welfare, CDSCO's primary mission is to protect and enhance public health. Within the CDSCO, the Drugs Controller General of India (DCGI) holds the highest regulatory authority for approving clinical trials in the country. The DCGI's role encompasses a wide range of responsibilities, including conducting inspections at trial sites, overseeing sponsors of clinical research, and monitoring manufacturing facilities related to pharmaceuticals and medical devices within India. Additionally, the DCGI provides leadership to institutions like the Central Drugs Testing Laboratory in Mumbai and the Regional Drugs Testing Laboratory[3].

Overall, the CDSCO and its pivotal regulatory figure, the DCGI, play a crucial role in ensuring the safety and efficacy of clinical trials and in upholding the quality of medical products in India[3], contributing significantly to the nation's healthcare standards. Similarly, regulatory bodies like the United States Food and Drug Administration (US FDA), Health Canada, and the European Medicines Agency function as counterparts abroad, collectively striving to safeguard public health and uphold stringent standards in the global healthcare landscape.

Indian Council of Medical Research (ICMR):

The Indian Council of Medical Research (ICMR) serves as the apex body responsible for the formulation, coordination, and promotion of biomedical research in India. This esteemed institution receives funding from the Ministry of Health and Family Welfare and operates under the purview of the Department of Health Research, Government of India.

ICMR has played a significant role in shaping the ethical conduct of biomedical and health research in the country. Over the years, it has released several key guidelines addressing the complex ethical considerations inherent in research involving human subjects. In 1980, the "Policy Statement on Ethical Considerations Involved in Research on Human Subjects" marked a significant milestone, followed by the publication of "Ethical Guidelines for Biomedical Research on Human Subjects" in 2000, and the revised version in 2006. These guidelines have been continuously updated to align

with the accelerated advancements in biomedical science and technology, ensuring the safety and welfare of research participants.

Drawing inspiration from international ethical frameworks such as the Nuremberg Code, the Declaration of Helsinki, and the Belmont Report, ICMR's guidelines incorporate universal ethical principles while considering India's diverse sociocultural ethos and varying healthcare standards. The revisions of the National Ethical Guidelines for Biomedical and Health Research Involving Human Participants in 2017 further expanded the scope of research areas covered. These guidelines now encompass public health research, social and behavioral sciences research for health, research during humanitarian emergencies and disasters, and responsible conduct of research. The revised ICMR ethical guidelines address emerging ethical issues and specialized areas such as the informed consent process, handling of biological materials, biobanking, datasets, and vulnerability. By doing so, ICMR continues to play a pivotal role in safeguarding the rights and well-being of research participants, promoting rigorous ethical standards, and fostering responsible and impactful biomedical research in India[4].

Clinical Research in India:

Clinical research can be broadly categorized into two main types based on how exposures are allocated: experimental and observational. If exposure (treatment) is assigned by the investigator then it would be experimental trial. Experimental trials fall under the purview of the New Drug Clinical Trials Rule (NDCTR 2019) and can further be classified into randomized and non-randomized trials. Randomized trials involve the random allocation of participants to different study groups, while non-randomized trials do not use random allocation. On the other hand, observational studies (exposure assigned by the treating physicians not by the investigators, investigators would only observe) are guided by the revised National Ethical Guidelines for Biomedical and Health Research Involving Human Participants 2017.

These studies can be either descriptive or analytical. Descriptive studies lack a control group and include investigations such as case-series reports. Analytical studies, on the other hand, incorporate a comparison (control) cohort. Cohort studies, a type of analytical study, monitor individuals over time from exposure to outcome. In contrast, case-control studies trace back from the outcome to the exposure. Additionally, cross-sectional studies capture both exposure and outcome at a single point in time, analogous to a snapshot. Researchers undertaking clinical research must ensure that experimental trials adhere to the NDCTR 2019, and observational studies follow the revised National Ethical Guidelines for Biomedical and Health Research Involving Human Participants 2017. These guidelines provide essential ethical frameworks to safeguard research participants and maintain the integrity and reliability of the research conducted[4, 5].

Schedule Y to the New Drugs and Clinical Trials Rules, 2019:

The transformation from Schedule Y to the New Drugs and Clinical Trials Rules, 2019 marked a significant milestone in India's efforts to align its regulations with internationally prevalent standards. The amendment to Schedule Y in 2005 was a crucial step towards harmonizing Indian clinical trial regulations with global practices. It introduced a clear definition of clinical trials and allowed for trials to be conducted in India during the same phase of drug development as in other countries. The 2005 amendment also emphasized the importance of informed consent, defined specific roles for sponsors, investigators, and ethics committee members, and mandated approval from the office of the Drugs Controller General of India (DCGI) for protocol amendments.

The Ministry of Health and Family Welfare released the comprehensive New Drugs and Clinical Trials Rules in 2019 to further promote clinical research in India. These new regulations covered various aspects, including provisions for orphan drugs, post-trial access, and pre- and post-submission meetings. The regulations were designed to raise ethical and quality standards in clinical trials,

benefiting both patients and the pharmaceutical industry. The New Rules, 2019 streamlined the review process for clinical trial applications, increased transparency and predictability in the regulatory pathway, and provided clarity on complex topics, such as post-trial access. Additionally, the regulations introduced expedited product approval under certain conditions, encouraging local drug development and enhancing the system's predictability and confidence.

The transformation from Schedule Y to the New Drugs and Clinical Trials Rules, 2019 was necessitated by concerns raised following media allegations of unethical practices in 2013. Stringent guidelines were introduced for conducting clinical trials, leaving sponsors conducting Global Clinical Trials (GCT) in India in a state of confusion and ambiguity. Despite efforts to overcome obstacles, the number of clinical trials approved by the Indian regulator did not reach previous levels. Consequently, the Central Drugs Standard Control Organisation (CDSCO) reexamined the regulations and introduced the New Drugs and Clinical Trials Rules, 2019 to revitalize clinical research in India. These new regulations aimed to address the challenges faced by sponsors, streamline the approval process, and reinforce India's position as a reliable destination for clinical trials while adhering to global ethical and quality standards[6].

New Drugs and Clinical Trials Rules 2019:

The New Drugs and Clinical Trials Rules 2019 brought significant changes to the regulation of biomedical and health research in India. Prior to these rules, certain types of studies, other than clinical trials and bioavailability and bioequivalence studies, were not adequately regulated under the Drug and Cosmetic Rules. These studies were covered by the Indian Council of Medical Research (ICMR) in the National Ethical Guidelines for Biomedical and Health Research Involving Human Participants, leading to ambiguity in the approval mechanism and compensation process. The New Rules, 2019 defined such research to include studies on basic, applied, and operational research or clinical research primarily focused on increasing scientific knowledge about diseases and conditions. Under the New Rules, 2019, various types of studies, including In Vitro Diagnostics (IVDs) performance testing, new surgical interventions, Assisted Reproductive Technology (ART), public health surveys, epidemiological health surveys, and observational and non-interventional studies of old drugs, are subject to approval by ethics committees registered under the Central Drugs Standard Control Organisation (CDSCO) as the "Ethics Committee for Biomedical and Health Research." These regulations not only aim to regulate such studies but also emphasize the importance of ethics committee oversight for ensuring subject safety and well-being[5].

The New Rules, 2019 also introduced the concept of academic clinical trials, which involve investigating a drug already approved for certain indications for new indications, routes of administration, doses, or dosage forms for academic or research purposes only, without seeking approval for marketing or commercial purposes. Ethics committees play a crucial role in academic clinical trials, ensuring adherence to approved protocols and ethical principles specified in the ICMR Guidelines for Biomedical Research on Human Participants. Academic clinical studies, whether Investigator Initiated Clinical Trials (IICT) or research conducted during post-graduate programmes in colleges, constitute the backbone of fundamental research. In the event of injury in Academic CT and Biomedical and Health Research (BHR), the Ethics Committee (EC) is responsible for determining the causality of Serious Adverse Events (SAE) and recommending appropriate compensation, while the host institution is responsible for providing compensation and/or covering compensation costs. However, it would be difficult for ECs to ascertain the amount of compensation because the ICMR Guidelines do not contain a formula for compensation calculation. Thus, it is imperative to develop guidelines for determining the amount of compensation[5]. Table 1 summarizes key features of academic clinical trial.

Additionally, the New Rules, 2019 included provisions for presubmission meetings between applicants, CDSCO officers, and subject experts to discuss the regulatory pathway for specific applications. This provision allows applicants to seek

Table 1: Key Points on Academic Clinical Trial (CT):
- This type of trial can be done only for approved drug
- CT initiated by investigator, academic or research institute can be conducted for new indication, new route, new dose or dosage form results only for academic or research purpose and not for commercial purpose.
- Data cannot be used for seeking approval in any country
- EC can seek clarity from Central Licensing Authority (CLA) and CLA must respond in 30 days (or deemed that no approval is needed)
- Medical management and compensation is applicable as per ICMR Guidelines for Biomedical Research on Human Participants
- Academic CTs are required to be conducted in accordance with the CT protocol approved by the EC and ethical principles specified in the ICMR Guidelines for Biomedical Research on Human Participants

guidance about the requirements and procedures for obtaining licenses or permissions for manufacturing processes, clinical trials, and other aspects related to biomedical research. The implementation of presubmission sessions under the new rules offers valuable benefits for companies planning regulatory submissions. This opportunity allows companies to engage in discussions with regulatory authorities to gain clarity and insights into the appropriate regulatory pathway for product registration. By seeking guidance before initiating the submission process, companies can better understand the requirements and expectations of the regulatory authority, reducing uncertainty and potential delays in the approval process.

Previously, companies had limited opportunities for discussions with regulatory officials, which sometimes led to ambiguities and challenges in understanding the necessary steps for product registration. With presubmission sessions now in place, companies can proactively address potential issues, avoid investing in unnecessary studies, and ensure that their research aligns with regulatory requirements. This change enhances communication between companies and regulators, fostering a more efficient and informed approach to product registration in the medical field.

Overall, the key changes introduced by the New Drugs and Clinical Trials Rules, 2019 aim to enhance the regulation and ethical oversight of biomedical and health research in India, ensuring patient safety, promoting academic research, and providing clarity on regulatory processes.

Revising the Definition of New Drug[5]:

The following were added to the definition of 'novel drugs': phytopharmaceutical medicines, novel drug delivery system of any drug from living modified organisms, monoclonal antibodies, stem cell-derived products, gene therapeutic products, or xenografts intended for use as drugs.

Two categories of new medications are distinguished. The first category would become an ancient drug four years after its approval, whereas the second category has always been designated "new drugs," regardless of how long ago they were first approved by the CLA. Class (i) belongs to the first category, while Classes (ii) and (iii) belong to the second category. The sustained release and modified release dosage formulations have been transferred to the second category. CTs and marketing approvals pertaining to the second category of products would legally fall under the jurisdiction of CLA. Even for generic products (after four years of innovator approval), local manufacturing requires approval from the CLA and then the State FDA. For sustained and modified release dosage forms, there would be additional timelines for generic product approval, as these dosage forms would first require CLA approval.

Phase IV Clinical Trial (CT) and post-marketing surveillance (PMS) studies[5]:

Under the 2019 New Drugs and Clinical Trials Rules, Phase IV CT and post-marketing surveillance (PMS) studies for new medications are now clearly defined with distinct requirements. Phase IV CT include investigations involving pharmaceutical combinations and dose-response or safety studies that support the use of medications according to their approved indications[5].

In Phase IV CT, ethical considerations are paramount to protect the rights, safety, and well-being of trial subjects. The regulatory provisions, including those related to compensation in the event of any injury or death resulting from the clinical trial, and the guidelines for good clinical practices are strictly adhered to. Study medications are typically provided to trial subjects at no cost, ensuring accessibility and ethical conduct. Any exceptions to providing medications at no cost must be specifically approved by the Central Licensing Authority (CLA) and the Ethics Committee (EC), accompanied by justifications or concerns. Table depicts types of different studies included in phase IV CT.

Table 2: Studies included in Phase IV CT

- drug-drug interactions
- dose-response or safety studies
- trials designed to support use under the approved indications

Postmarketing surveillance (PMS) studies, on the other hand, focus on monitoring the safety and effectiveness of medications once they are already on the market. These studies are critical for gathering real-world data and detecting any potential adverse effects that may have gone unnoticed during earlier clinical trials. By actively monitoring medications during their postmarketing phase, regulatory authorities can take prompt actions to ensure patient safety and well-being.

Both Phase IV studies and postmarketing surveillance play essential roles in evaluating the long-term safety and effectiveness of medications, allowing continuous improvement in patient care and regulatory decision-making. These studies are essential components of the drug development and monitoring process, contributing to public health and patient safety.

Orphan Drugs:

The 2019 New Drugs and Clinical Trials Rules define orphan pharmaceuticals as drugs intended to treat conditions that affect fewer than five lakh

(500,000) people in India. To foster research and development of orphan medications, the New Rules, 2019 introduce several favorable provisions. Orphan drugs receive special status, expedited approval, and a complete clinical trial filing fee waiver. Additionally, an expedited evaluation procedure is available for cases where clinical safety and efficacy have been demonstrated, allowing for accelerated approval even if all phases of clinical trials have not been completed. However, postmarketing studies may be required to validate anticipated clinical benefits after accelerated approval.

In contrast, the United States' Orphan Drug Designation program grants orphan status to pharmaceuticals and biologics intended to treat diseases affecting fewer than 200,000 people. The US program also provides a list of rare diseases based on country regulations. Similarly, the Central Drugs Standard Control Organisation (CDSCO) in India should consider devising a similar method for listing rare diseases based on Indian registry data. This list of rare diseases may be subject to periodic review if deemed necessary by the Central Licensing Authority (CLA). These provisions aim to promote the development of orphan drugs, address unmet medical needs, and enhance patient access to treatments for rare conditions in India[5].

Post-Trial Access:

Post-trial access is a critical aspect of clinical research that pertains to providing trial subjects with continued access to a new drug or investigational new drug after the completion of a clinical trial. As per the 2019 New Drugs and Clinical Trials Rules in India, post-trial access is granted when the drug has been found beneficial to the trial subject and is deemed necessary by the investigator and ethics committee. This provision ensures that trial subjects who have benefited from the investigational drug during the study are not deprived of continued treatment once the trial is completed. Importantly, post-trial access should be provided at no cost to the trial subjects, ensuring equitable access to potentially beneficial medications. However, certain

aspects regarding post-trial access still warrant further clarification. For instance, the duration of post-trial access, particularly for chronic diseases requiring long-term treatment, remains open to interpretation. Additionally, there is a need to define specific procedures for safety signal monitoring during this period, and the responsibilities of sponsors, investigators, and ethics committees in recording and reporting safety issues after the study concludes should be outlined. Moreover, the question of whether sponsors should continue to provide post-trial access after the drug receives marketing authorization and becomes commercially available requires careful consideration. To address these concerns and maintain ethical standards, it is recommended that distinct guidelines governing post-trial access to pharmaceuticals be established, providing clarity and consistency in this crucial aspect of clinical research. In conclusion, post-trial access is a vital component of ethical clinical research, ensuring that trial subjects who have benefited from investigational drugs have continued access to potentially life-saving treatments. To uphold patient welfare and research integrity, further guidance from regulatory authorities on post-trial access is essential. Defining clear guidelines will foster transparency, promote patient well-being, and strengthen the overall ethical framework of clinical trials in India.

Ethics Committee[5]:

Ethics Committees (ECs) play a pivotal role in ensuring the ethical conduct of biomedical and health research in accordance with the 2019 New Drugs and Clinical Trials Rules. The new regulations introduce several significant requirements for EC composition and operations. Each EC must have at least one female member to promote gender diversity and representation. Moreover, to maintain independence and impartiality, 50% of the EC members must not be affiliated with the institution or organization that formed the committee. This provision aims to prevent conflicts of interest and strengthen the integrity of the review process.

Furthermore, the new regulations mandate regular training and development programs for EC members, ensuring that they remain updated on evolving ethical guidelines and best practices. Any changes in the membership or constitution of a registered EC must be promptly disclosed in writing to the Central Licensing Authority (CLA) within 30 working days, fostering transparency and accountability. Before undertaking the review of any new clinical trials, ECs must undergo reconstitution to align with the updated regulations, followed by re-registration to ensure compliance. For the evaluation of biomedical and health research proposals, ECs are required to register with the designated authority under the Department of Health Research, within the Ministry of Health (MoH). Initially, provisional registration with a two-year validity period is granted, allowing ECs to commence their operations. Upon a thorough review of the submitted documentation and adherence to the regulatory requirements, the designated authority may grant a final registration using Form CT-03. These measures aim to streamline the registration process and enhance the effectiveness and accountability of ECs in safeguarding the welfare and rights of research participants.

Increased Fees for various applications:

The regulatory landscape for clinical trials in India has witnessed fee increases for various applications under the 2019 New Drugs and Clinical Trials Rules. Notably, application fees for Phase III Clinical Trials have risen significantly from INR 25,000 to INR 200,000, reflecting a substantial increase. Additionally, Phase IV studies, which were previously exempt from fees, now require an application fee of INR 200,000. Moreover, new categories have emerged, such as the fee for CLA reconsideration of a denied application, further adding to the financial burden for applicants[5].

However, certain entities benefit from reduced or waived fees. Government entities conducting clinical trials are exempt from fees, promoting research initiatives by public organizations.

Similarly, Micro, Small, and Medium Enterprises (MSME) are eligible for a 50% reduction in application fees for various clinical trial-related activities, including approval of new medicines, presubmission and post-submission meetings. Notably, no application fees apply to clinical trials involving orphan medicines, encouraging research and development in this critical area. Although the increased fees may raise concerns among applicants, it is crucial to consider the potential benefits. The revised fee structure is expected to assist the government in offsetting costs associated with increasing personnel and enhancing regulatory capabilities. This, in turn, aims to expedite the review process and facilitate oversight of an ever-growing number of clinical trial applications and sites more effectively. While the fee adjustments may present challenges, the potential gains in regulatory efficiency and improved patient safety and welfare are essential considerations for stakeholders in the clinical research community[5].

Waivers of local clinical trial data:

The 2019 New Drugs and Clinical Trials Rules in India outline provisions for waivers of local clinical trial data requirements, aiming to facilitate the importation and approval to manufacture new medicines in the country. Rule 75 sets the conditions for waiving local clinical trial requirements for the importation of new drugs. Such waivers may be granted if the drug is approved and marketed in specific countries specified by the licensing authority, and if a global clinical trial involving the drug is ongoing in India, with interim approval in certain countries listed by the licensing authority and no reports of major unexpected serious adverse events. Additionally, the waiver implementation necessitates that there is no probability or evidence of significant differences in the Indian population's enzymes or genes related to the drug's metabolism or any factors affecting its pharmacokinetics, pharmacodynamics, safety, and efficacy.

In these cases, the applicant must conduct a Phase IV study based on a design approved by the Central Licensing Authority (CLA). However, for drugs indicated for life-threatening or serious diseases, diseases of special relevance to the Indian health scenario, conditions with unmet needs in India, rare diseases with limited availability or high costs for drugs, or orphan drugs, the requirement for a Phase IV study may be waived. Moreover, data submission requirements for certain animal studies may be relaxed for novel pharmaceuticals with at least two years of approval and marketing in other countries.

Rule 80 outlines similar conditions for waiving local clinical trial requirements for the approval to manufacture new medicines (local products). The conditions mirror those for the importation of new drugs, except that the submission of data from certain animal studies, such as toxicology, reproduction, teratogenicity, perinatality, mutagenicity, and carcinogenicity studies, may be modified or relaxed for new drugs that have been approved and marketed in other countries for a specific period. These provisions enable regulatory authorities in India to evaluate and certify new drugs based on their approval and performance data from other countries. By allowing for these waivers, the process of drug approval and availability in India can be expedited, reducing the time between global drug launches and patients' access to much-needed medications in the country. This flexibility in data requirements also encourages pharmaceutical companies to bring innovative and life-saving treatments to India's healthcare landscape more efficiently, benefiting patients in need of these novel therapies[5, 6].

Import and Manufacture of Unapproved new Drug:

The 2019 New Drugs and Clinical Trials Rules in India introduced provisions for patients to seek a license to import and manufacture unapproved new drugs, providing potential avenues for accessing life-saving treatments.

Under Rule 36 of the Drugs and Cosmetics Rules, 1945, patients can apply for a license to import an unapproved new medicine. The applicant must submit a Form 12A application, along with a prescription from a Registered Medical Practitioner (RMP), indicating the required quantity of the medication for the patient's treatment. The authorization in the form of Form 12B is prioritized, subject to the relevant supporting documentation and approval from the Licensing Authority (LA). Notably, medical professionals from government hospitals are now also permitted to import unapproved pharmaceuticals that have obtained marketing approval in their country of origin under the 2019 New Rules. This provision is particularly beneficial for individuals suffering from major, life-threatening illnesses, permanent disabilities, or unmet medical needs, offering them access to potentially life-saving medications that are not yet approved in India[5].

Moreover, the New Rules also include a provision for the manufacture of experimental new drugs that have not yet received regulatory approval in India. These drugs can be produced in small quantities solely for the purpose of treating patients with life-threatening illnesses. This step aims to provide critically ill patients with access to promising and innovative treatments that are still undergoing clinical trials and awaiting formal approval. Overall, these provisions open up new possibilities for patients to access essential medications and experimental treatments, granting them hope and potential therapeutic options in challenging medical situations.

Expedited licensing of novel drugs:
The 2019 New Drugs and Clinical Trials Rules (NDCTR) in India include a crucial clause that allows for the expedited licensing of novel drugs specifically intended to treat medical conditions of particular significance to India or address urgent medical needs, especially in times of disasters or for specific defense purposes.

This provision is aimed at accelerating the approval process for drugs that hold great potential for the Indian population's health and well-being, particularly in critical situations. In such cases, if exceptional effectiveness is observed based on Phase II clinical evidence, marketing authorization may be granted without the need to complete all phases of clinical trials. This expedited licensing is a significant step in responding swiftly to medical emergencies and addressing pressing healthcare challenges that affect the Indian population, ensuring access to promising treatments in a timely manner[5].

However, it is important to note that despite the expedited licensing, the NDCTR 2019 emphasizes the importance of scientific rigor and safety. To ensure the drug's effectiveness and safety in the long term, a Phase IV clinical study will be required under these exceptional circumstances. This follow-up study aims to confirm any predicted therapeutic advantages observed in Phase II and to gather further evidence on the drug's real-world performance and potential side effects. The inclusion of this Phase IV clinical study requirement demonstrates the authorities' commitment to upholding high-quality research and patient safety while responding promptly to urgent medical needs and catastrophic situations. This provision is a significant advancement in streamlining drug approval processes in India, enabling faster access to novel treatments that hold promise for improving public health and addressing critical medical challenges in the country.

Restricted Use in Emergency[7]:

In response to novel pandemics and public health emergencies, the Central Drug Standard Control Organization (CDSCO) in India has implemented an accelerated approval pathway known as "Restricted Use in Emergency". This pathway was formally established under the New Drugs and Clinical Trials (NDCT) rules 2019, falling under the Drugs and Cosmetic Act 1940 and Rules 1945. Before this, India did not have a formal expedited pathway to respond to public health emergencies. The CDSCO introduced this accelerated approval process to address the surge in COVID-19 cases in India, enabling the quick authorization of certain drugs and the formal notification for the manufacture of novel vaccines.

Under the restricted emergency use authorization, foreign-produced COVID-19 vaccines that have already been approved by regulatory agencies like USFDA, EMA, UKMHRA, and PMDA, or are WHO-listed for emergency use, can be granted permission for restricted use in India. The regulatory process for approval is expedited, and the Drug Controller General of India (DCGI) makes the decision on granting permission for restricted emergency use within three working days from the submission date of the application. Once approved, the applicant is required to initiate a clinical trial within 30 days, and the first 100 recipients of the vaccine are assessed for seven days to evaluate safety before launching the vaccination program. CDSCO evaluates the application at the highest priority and provides guidance on the regulatory pathway if needed. The safety data submitted by the applicant is thoroughly reviewed, and once found satisfactory, the applicant is authorized to use the vaccine under the COVID-19 vaccination program.

This expedited authorization pathway ensures that critical medications and vaccines can be swiftly made available to address public health emergencies in India. The process allows for a rapid response to urgent healthcare needs while maintaining necessary safety standards and monitoring through rigorous assessment and evaluation. The use of this pathway has been instrumental in facilitating the import and use of foreign-produced COVID-19 vaccines that have received approvals from reputable international regulatory authorities, helping to combat the COVID-19 pandemic effectively in the country[8].

Timelines for the approval of new clinical trials:

The New Drugs and Clinical Trials Rules (NDCTR) 2019 in India have introduced specific timelines for the approval of new clinical trials. For medications developed outside of India, the Central Licensing Authority (CLA) has a maximum of 90 working days to respond to the application for clinical trials. However, in cases where the medicine was discovered in India, is currently undergoing research and development there, and is intended to be produced and marketed within the country, the review period may be further expedited to just 30 working days. This streamlined timeline aims to support and encourage the development of new medications within India and foster the growth of the domestic pharmaceutical industry.

For studies involving bioavailability/ bioequivalence (BA/BE) of new medications or investigational new pharmaceuticals, an automatic presumption of authorization is granted if no response is received from the CLA within 90 working days of the application receipt. This provision aims to expedite the approval process for such studies, facilitating quicker access to critical research data and supporting the efficient development and evaluation of new pharmaceutical products. These specified timelines under NDCTR 2019 demonstrate the Indian regulatory authority's commitment to promoting timely and efficient evaluation of new clinical studies, encouraging both domestic and international research and development initiatives within the country[5].

Irrespective of the nature of the new drug, a pre-submission consultation may be held with the FDA if required. The type of submission required and the authority to accord such approval varies from case to case[5]. A description of various submission types are detailed below:

Clinical Trials
- New drugs - application to be submitted in CT-04 and approval in CT-06
- application to be reviewed within 90 working days; for a drug discovered and researched in India, application to be reviewed within 30 working days

- Marketed drugs – no approval required from CDSCO, only EC approval required
- Phytopharmaceuticals – to be conducted as per applicable rules and guidelines for new drugs
- Academic clinical study – no approval required from CDSCO, only EC approval is required
- Biomedical and Health Research – approval required from Ethics Committee registered under Rule 17
- BA/BE study – application to be submitted in CT-05 and approval in CT-07
- application to be reviewed within 90 working days
- Import or Manufacture of New Drug
- For either import or manufacture of new drug, if requirements for waiver of local clinical trial are met, the application for marketing authorization can be submitted.
- For Import, application has to be submitted in CT-18 and approval is given in CT-19 for API and CT-20 for finished formulation. Application review timeline is 90 days in this case.
- For manufacture of new drug, application has to be submitted in CT-21. Approval is given in CT-22 for API or CT-22 for finished formulation. Application review timeline is 90 working days.

International Regulations:

The globalisation of medication development has highlighted the significance of harmonisation and cooperation across drug regulatory authorities. Among these, the US Food and Drug Administration (FDA) and the European Medicines Agency (EMA) are two key players frequently compared in terms of their assessment timelines for marketing applications. To facilitate global alignment while considering regional requirements, it is essential to understand the variations in the expectations and standards of drug development and safety evaluation employed by these regulatory agencies. Comparing and analysing the judgements made about applications can shed light on how they utilize regulatory science. Both the FDA and EMA are committed to advancing international synchronisation of reliable regulatory standards in drug development, and they participate in the International Council for Harmonisation of Technical Requirements for Pharmaceuticals for Human Use (ICH) to ensure the safety, efficiency, and quality of pharmaceutical products. Over the past decade, they have established platforms for information exchange and collaboration through standing working groups, focusing on various aspects of medical drug product development and regulation. Although specific product decisions are made within their respective legal frameworks, discussions on regulatory science serve as a foundation for aligning high-impact standards and approaches[9].

The regulation of medical medicines and devices (DADs) while ensuring timely access to novel treatments is a complex balancing act undertaken by regulatory authorities worldwide. In the United States, the Federal Food and Drug Administration (FDA) and in the European Union (EU), regional and centralised regulatory organisations primarily bear this responsibility. However, differences in their regulatory processes, timelines, and prices have been a subject of contention. Critics have accused the FDA of slow and risk-averse approval procedures, which they argue hinder American citizens from accessing effective DADs available in Europe. Conversely, concerns about rapid authorisations endangering patient safety have been raised in the EU. Calls for regulatory consistency and tighter approval procedures have emerged, reflecting the ongoing efforts to find a balance between ensuring access to innovative treatments and ensuring patient safety.

The history of the FDA dates back to the 19th century when it was initially established to ensure the efficacy of drugs sold to the public. Over time, its authority expanded to include the regulation of medical devices in 1976, bolstered by the Medical Device User Fee and Modernization Act of 2002, granting more stringent powers to ensure both effectiveness and safety. Despite regulatory changes to expedite the DAD development process, the FDA's authority has remained largely unchanged across all 50 states since the 1970s.

In contrast, the development of European DAD legislation has been more recent, evolving after the creation of the EU in 1993. Before that, individual member nations were responsible for DAD regulation and marketing authorisation, leading to disparities in regulations and hindrances to cross-border distribution. Reorganisations among the 30 EEA countries (27 EU Member States plus Iceland, Liechtenstein and Norway) have sought to address these challenges, with clinical trial applications typically managed at the member state level and marketing applications requiring authorisation from both state and central organisations in accordance with EC requirements[10].

European regulations on Drug Development:

The European regulation of drugs encompasses various procedures to ensure the safe and efficient approval and marketing of medicinal products across EU member states. One of the key approaches is the centralised procedure, managed by the European Medicines Agency (EMA), which grants a single licence recognized by all EU members for specific drug classes, including treatments for HIV/AIDS, cancer, diabetes, neurodegenerative disorders, autoimmune illnesses, and viral diseases. This harmonized process streamlines drug approval, reduces costs for pharmaceutical companies, and eliminates barriers to competition within the EU market. However, it's important to note that each member state may also have its own procedures for licensing medicines, not subject to the centralised process. This decentralized approach allows individual EU countries to have their own review and approval mechanisms, giving them more flexibility to tailor regulations to their specific needs. Another significant aspect of the European drug regulation is mutual acknowledgment. Once a drug has received national approval in one EU member state, it can be granted marketing authorization in other EU member states. This mutual recognition system ensures that once a medicine has been thoroughly reviewed and approved in one country, other member states can acknowledge the validity of that decision, accelerating the process of making the drug available to patients across the EU.

Additionally, there is the decentralized procedure for drugs that have not yet received authorization in any EU member state and are not eligible for the required centralised process. Manufacturers can submit simultaneous applications for clearance in several EU states through this method. This decentralised approach has become increasingly popular and handles a large number of applications for approval.

Overall, the European regulation of drugs combines centralised, mutual acknowledgment, and decentralized procedures to create a comprehensive framework for drug approval and marketing within the EU. By harmonizing standards, facilitating mutual acknowledgment, and offering decentralized options, the EU aims to ensure that safe and effective medicines are readily available to patients across member states, while also promoting innovation and competition in the pharmaceutical industry[11].

Comparison between FDA and the EU drug approval processes[10, 12]:

The drug approval processes of the FDA and the EU have drawn attention for their differences in two key areas: the time taken for approvals and the availability of data from unpublished clinical studies.

Firstly, the concept to market period in both regions is crucial as it directly impacts the time and costs associated with bringing a drug or device to market. In Europe, there have been suggestions to expedite market entry after Phase II clinical studies, followed by post-market monitoring for ongoing safety and efficacy evaluation. On the other hand, there is a common perception that FDA protocols should be eased to speed up drug approval and align drug availability in Europe and the United States. However, a closer examination reveals that the FDA actually has faster drug approval timelines compared to the EMA. Studies have shown that the FDA's median review times for first reviews and comprehensive reviews of comparable medications were shorter than those of the EMA.

Furthermore, the US often saw the release of medications first, sometimes up to 90 days earlier than in Europe. This was particularly evident in cancer medications, where the US had access to a greater number of approved drugs and experienced reduced review times compared to the EMA[12].

Secondly, the transparency of data on drug approvals differs between the FDA and the EMA. Both regulatory bodies have expressed concerns about the lack of transparency in trial data, which hampers systematic reviews and meta-analyses critical for public health and safety. The FDA has taken steps to address this issue by making non-public data from new drug applications available online or upon request. The methodological quality of unpublished investigations has been found to be similar to published trials, indicating their relevance for systematic reviews. In contrast, the EMA considers unpublished data as "commercially sensitive" and does not readily share it with the public, unless there is a compelling public interest. This lack of data availability has been a subject of contention, and efforts to obtain unpublished study data from the EMA have faced challenges.

In summary, the FDA and the EU have distinct contrasts in their drug approval processes. While the concept to market period and transparency of data are areas of concern and debate, both regulatory bodies continuously work towards enhancing drug safety, efficacy, and accessibility for patients while adhering to their specific regulatory frameworks and considerations. Understanding these differences is crucial for stakeholders in the pharmaceutical industry, clinicians, and patients to navigate the complexities of drug development and approval in both regions.

Emergency use authorization (EUA) by USFDA: Emergency Use Authorization (EUA) is a critical authority granted to the US Food and Drug Administration (FDA) commissioner, enabling the issuance of an EUA under specific emergency circumstances.

These emergencies may be classified as domestic, public health, military, or related to a physical threat. The relevant secretary for the respective region or industry is involved in making decisions regarding EUA, following Section 564 of the Federal Food, Drug, and Cosmetic Act. The FDA commissioner consults with various departments and secretaries, including the National Institutes of Health, the Department of Health and Human Services (HHS), the Centers for Disease Control and Prevention, and the Assistant Secretary for Preparedness and Response, before granting the EUA. All relevant information regarding the EUA is made public in the federal registry.

The EUA process is based on a thorough assessment of data from preclinical and clinical investigations, considering factors such as effectiveness, intended usage, and benefit-risk ratio. This accelerated process is particularly important during emergencies, as the standard marketing approval procedure takes a considerable amount of time. The EUA mandates healthcare providers, including hospitals, to maintain detailed records of the allocation and dispensing of authorized medications, outlining how the medicine should be used, who will receive it, delivery methods, and frequency of use. Medications under EUA must adhere to strict labeling regulations, avoiding any claims of being safe and effective for the current emergency without extensive studies in complex medical conditions. The informed consent form, provided to patients by healthcare providers, plays a crucial role in the EUA process[13].

The EUA jurisdiction allows for the facilitation of medication and medical countermeasure supply during pandemics or public health emergencies (PHE). The HHS secretary declared a PHE on February 4, 2020, during the COVID-19 pandemic, highlighting the significance of such authorizations in addressing national security and protecting US citizens both domestically and abroad. However, it is important to note that medications and biologics approved under the EUA pathway cannot be used in post-emergency situations. For continued use, applicants must pursue the FDA's conventional drug approval process, involving the submission of investigational new drug (IND) and new drug application (NDA) forms for investigational and new

medications, respectively. The FDA retains the authority to revoke the EUA if necessary and appropriate, ensuring ongoing safety and regulation of medical products during emergencies.

Conditional Marketing Authorization (CMA) by European Union:

Conditional Marketing Authorization (CMA) is a vital mechanism in the European Union's medical product approval process, facilitated by the European Medicines Agency (EMA) and its scientific bodies like the Committee for Medical Products for Human Use (CHMP) and the Pharmacovigilance Risk Assessment Committee. The EU's quick approval procedure for medicines, biologics (vaccines), and therapies, including those for COVID-19, focuses on safety and risk reduction while supporting research and development. The CMA process involves four steps: rolling reviews, applications for CMA, evaluations by the EMA's scientific committee, and a decision-making process by the EMA to grant or deny CMA[14].

During public health emergencies (PHE) or pandemics, the EMA initiates a rolling review of clinical data for potential drugs, allowing for quick evaluation as new data becomes available. When all clinical data are validated and available, the sponsor can formally submit a Marketing Authorization Application (MAA) for CMA consideration. CMA is crucial in saving lives during PHEs by rapidly approving medications and biologicals through a fast-track authorization process, especially for highly infectious or fatal diseases with unmet medical needs. The acceptance of CMA depends on the favorable benefit-risk ratio of the medicine, the availability of future clinical data, and the importance of providing immediate access to patients despite incomplete data. Approved pharmaceuticals and biologics initially have a one-year expiration date for CMA, which can be renewed annually. The marketing authorization holder must fulfill specific requirements within the given timeframe to convert CMA into a regular centralised MAA, demonstrating continued favorable benefit-risk profile after evaluating additional accumulated data[15].

CMA-approved medicines and biologics are listed and published by the EMA in the European Public Assessment Report. In emergencies, sponsors may receive CMA without any conditions for up to five years, which can then be compared to regular marketing authorization and extended indefinitely. However, if new information reveals that the benefits no longer outweigh the risks or if the sponsor fails to meet regulatory requirements, the EMA may take regulatory action, such as suspending or revoking the marketing authorization. During the COVID-19 pandemic, CMA played a significant role in facilitating mass vaccination programs and ensuring simultaneous access to safe and effective COVID-19 vaccines for EU residents[14, 15].

Applicants seeking CMA are advised to set up pre-submission meetings with EMA to discuss their development goals and receive scientific advice or protocol support. The application for CMA must be mentioned in both their notice and the request. The applicant has a timeframe of six to seven months to submit the request before filing the MAA. Unlike regular marketing authorization, applicants are not required to submit the complete data postauthorization for unusual conditions of authorization. The CMA process serves as a valuable tool to expedite access to essential medications during emergencies while ensuring the ongoing evaluation of their safety and efficacy[15].

Continuing challenges to drug and device regulation and approval:

Continuing challenges persist in both the European Union (EU) and the United States regarding the regulation and approval of drugs and medical devices, as they strive to balance the assurance of safety and efficacy against the pressure from industry and the public to expedite the introduction of new products to the market. One of the major issues faced by both regions is the requirement for appropriate and efficient evidence standards for device clearance. In the US, only a small percentage of medical devices undergo premarket approval (PMA), which is the most stringent procedure for FDA device approval. Instead, many devices are cleared under the less rigorous 501(k) procedure. This raises concerns about the lack of clinical data and safety guarantees for certain devices. Similarly,

in the EU, regulations do not mandate comprehensive clinical trials to prove the therapeutic effectiveness of devices, leading to potential approval of devices without significant improvements or proper safety assessment. Post-market surveillance of safety and efficacy is another significant challenge in both the EU and the US. The FDA plays a central role in gathering and assessing adverse event data, and it has the authority to require post-marketing studies and specify the format of these studies. The FDA can also revoke the marketing authorization and demand the recall of a harmful device. In contrast, the EU conducts post-market surveillance through "vigilance systems," with adverse drug reactions being reported to the Competent Authority of each member country. However, penalties for noncompliance vary among member nations, making it difficult to compare rates of unsafe devices and interventions. The lack of transparency regarding data submitted for clinical approval and the absence of a central "clearing house" in the EU further complicate the assessment of device safety. The industry's resistance to proposals for centralizing device approval procedures in the EU adds to the challenges, despite potential benefits in uniformity and patient safety. Collaboration between the European Medicines Agency (EMA) and the FDA aims to address medication safety, and there have been proposals for changes to medical device regulations in the EU. However, challenges persist, and it remains uncertain when new regulations will be approved. Overall, both the EU and the US grapple with striking the right balance between ensuring the safety and efficacy of drugs and devices while meeting demands for quicker access to new treatments. The need for robust evidence standards, effective post-market surveillance, and harmonization of regulations are critical areas that require ongoing attention to improve patient safety and access to innovative medical products[16].

Conclusion:
In conclusion, the field of clinical research is constantly evolving, with regulations playing a crucial role in ensuring patient safety and promoting innovation. In India, the recent amendments to the regulations demonstrate a commitment to raising ethical and quality standards for clinical trials, which will benefit both the pharmaceutical industry and

patients. The streamlined approval process for indigenous medicines and the potential for early access to medications will foster local drug development and attract more international clinical trials to the country. On a global scale, the United States and the European Union remain at the forefront of medical device and drug research and approval. Despite differences in their regulatory histories, both regions share the common goal of balancing safety and efficacy while advancing medical advancements. Collaborative efforts between the US and the EU reflect a growing recognition of the need for mutual standardization and openness in the approval process for medical devices.

As the landscape of clinical research continues to evolve, it is essential for all stakeholders, including academic researchers, regulatory bodies, and pharmaceutical sectors, to work together cohesively. This collaboration should aim to ensure consistent and high-quality review processes while prioritizing patient protection and risk-benefit assessment. Ultimately, a harmonized approach to clinical research regulations on a global scale will lead to more efficient drug and device approval processes, benefitting patients worldwide. As stakeholders continue to refine and improve regulatory frameworks, we can expect to see continued progress in the field of clinical research, leading to better healthcare outcomes and increased access to life-saving medications and medical devices for patients everywhere.

References:

1. Paul SM, Mytelka DS, Dunwiddie CT, Persinger CC, Munos BH, Lindborg SR, et al. How to improve R and D productivity: The pharmaceutical industry's grand challenge. Nat Rev Drug Discov. 2010;9:203–14.
2. Gogtay NJ, Ravi R, Thatte UM. Regulatory requirements for clinical trials in India: What academicians need to know. Indian J Anaesth. 2017 Mar;61(3):192-199. doi: 10.4103/ija.IJA_143_17. PMID: 28405032; PMCID: PMC5372399.
3. Central Drugs Standard Control Organization. [Last accessed on 2023 July 20]. Available from: https://www.cdscoonline.gov.in/CDSCO/homepage .
4. Indian Council of Medical Research. National Ethical Guidelines for Biomedical and Health Research Involving Human Participants. New Delhi; 2017. https://icmr.nic.in/guidelines/ICMR_Ethical_Guidelines_2017.pdf. Accessed 20 July 2023.
5. G.S.R.227(E). New Drugs and Clinical Trials Rules, 2019. Ministry of Health and Family Welfare, India. March 2019. http://www.egazette.nic.in/WriteReadData/2019/200759.pdf. Accessed 20 July 2023.
6. Jain P and Chauhan R. "India's New Drugs and Clinical Trials Rules: An Industry Perspective." Regulatory Focus. July 2019. Regulatory Affairs Professionals Society.
7. Bhave AC. Indian regulatory update during the COVID-19 pandemic. Perspect Clin Res 2020;11:132-4
8. Bishnoi, Mamta; Sonker, Aniket. Emergency use authorization of medicines: History and ethical dilemma. Perspectives in Clinical Research 14(2):p 49-55, Apr–Jun 2023. | DOI: 10.4103/picr.picr_149_22
9. Downing, N.S., Zhang, A.D. & Ross, J.S. Regulatory review of new therapeutic agents — FDA versus EMA, 2011–2015. N. Engl. J. Med. 376, 1386–1387 (2017)
10. Van Norman GA. Drugs and Devices: Comparison of European and U.S. Approval Processes. JACC Basic Transl Sci. 2016 Aug 29;1(5):399-412. doi: 10.1016/j.jacbts.2016.06.003. PMID: 30167527; PMCID: PMC6113412.
11. Kashyap U.N., Gupta V., Raghunandan H.V. Comparison of drug approval process in United States and Europe. J Pharm Sci Res. 2013;5:131–136.
12. Downing N.S., Aminawung J.A., Shah N. Regulatory review of novel therapeutics—comparison of three regulatory agencies. N Engl J Med. 2012;366:2284–2293.
13. Zuckerman DM. Emergency use authorizations (EUAs) versus FDA approval:Implications for COVID-19 and public health. Am J Public Health 2021;111:1065-9
14. Hidalgo-Simon A, Botgros R, Cochino E. Authorization of vaccines in the European Union. Mol Front J 2021;5:58-65

15. Cavaleri M, Enzmann H, Straus S, Cooke E. The European Medicines Agency's EU conditional marketing authorisations for COVID-19 vaccines. Lancet 2021;397:355-7

16. Eichler HG, Pgnatti F, Flamion B, Leufkens H, Breckenridge A. Balancing early market access to new drugs with the need for benefit/risk data: an mounting dilemma. Nat Rev Drug Discov 2008;7:818–26.

Chapter 04

New Drug Clinical Trial Rule-2019— A brief update

Sri Somanath Basu
Scientist E, Ex-Deputy Drug Controller/Technical Officer, CDSCO, Govt of India.
Currently, QMS and Regulatory affairs, Andrapradesh MedTech Zone Limited,
Vishakapatnam, Andrapradesh

Abstract

March 2019, just one year before SARS CoV-2 became pandemic around the world, Health ministry of Union of India published a new comprehensive set of Rules and guidelines namely "New drugs and Clinical Trial Rule-2019". The rule was notified by Govt. of India as effective on the very date of it's publication on 19 March 2019. A brief update on origin and previous versions of NDCT 2019 is discussed in this article. Remaining details are discussed by subsequent authors in their respective articles.

March 2019, just one year before SARS CoV-2 became pandemic around the world, Health ministry of Union of India published a new comprehensive set of Rules and guidelines namely "New drugs and Clinical Trial Rule-2019". The rule was notified by Govt. of India as effective on the very date of it's publication on 19 March 2019.

Prior to this NDCT-2019, the approval process of new drugs was executed under schedule-Y, which was a set of guideline accompanied by some set of Rules under Drugs and Cosmetics Rule - 1945. Schedule-Y was inserted in the Drugs and Cosmetics Rule – 1945 in late 80's under the able stewardship of the then DCG(I) Dr. P. Dasgupta M.D. (pharmacology). During that phase some rDNA drug products e.g. Insulin, EPO were yet to be introduced in the Indian market. The concerns of Ethics committees, BA / BE study centers and clinical trials on New drugs were just emerging. There were no clause for paying compensation in cases if Serious Adverse Events (SAE).

The concerns were also put under public litigation alleging the Indian patients were being treated as Guinea pigs for testing of medicines and there were no laws protecting the patient's interest etc.

One NGO Swasthya Sewa Manch of Bhopal (MP) filed litigation in Supreme Court of India in this regard, they were heard by the bench of hon'ble justice Lodha in various sessions and accordingly final verdict came directing Govt. Of India to publish separate set of comprehensive Rules under the sentinel Drugs and Cosmetics Act 1940 which was enacted pre-independence of India by the British Government.

Introduction of NDCT 2019: This set of Rule is now created including 8 chapters comprising of definitions of various clinical trial related technologies, regulation of Ethics Committees involved in human trial with new medicines & biomedical health research aspects. Import & manufacture of new medicines for clinical trial purposes and commercialization in the country. One miscellaneous chapter has been created enabling the manufacturers and importers with certain provisions for pre & post approval hearing with the national regulatory agency (CDSCO-HQ), preserving the interests of stakeholders who had already obtained various licenses, permissions etc. from CDSCO.

Corre-
sponding author: Sri Somanath Basu. Can be contacted at phone no. 98104 92954

5th schedule is inserted in NDCT-2019 Rule for guidance to the stakeholders regarding post market approval surveillance of new medicines including the documentation details of PSUR (Periodic safety update Reports), mentioning active & passive surveillance, RMP (Risk management plan), RSI (Reference safety information) . However, the biggest challenge still remains that there is no compulsory provisions under Drugs and Cosmetics Act and Rules made there under to follow up all other chemical origin medicines which are placed in Indian market for more than 4- years, for example cough syrup with combination of various active ingredients e.g. pholcodine. Under these circumstances, govt. has no other options but to depend the adverse reactions reported from other countries, WHO database etc.

In 3rd schedule of NDCT rule, the points to be covered under Prescribing Information (PI) are highlighted. But this is for new medicines only. Obviously, this guidance on prescribing information should also be maintained for all medicines. However in this direction, a law statement should have been there.

The best features in NDCT rule as it transforms from its precursor schedule-Y is that for every activity on part of the regulatory agency, a time line has been formulated and mandated by a Law statement. To avoid ambiguities, many common terms frequently used in drug regulations have been defined in first chapter. Tables guidance are provided for preparing SAE reporting, Investigators Brochure, clinical trial reporting, Application for EC registration, detailed compensation calculation etc. are also presented in NDCT.

Chapter 05

Protocol Components and Clinical Trial Design

Dr Suyog Sindhu MBBS MD, FAIMER (2020), MFILIPE,
Associate Professor, Department of Pharmacology and Therapeutics,
King George's Medical University,
Lucknow, Uttar Pradesh

Abstract

Clinical trials are crucial for advancing medical knowledge and improving patient care globally, including in India. Designing effective protocols that address the unique challenges and considerations in both international and Indian contexts is essential. This write-up provides a comprehensive overview of protocol components and common challenges encountered in clinical trial design, considering both international guidelines, such as the International Council for Harmonisation of Technical Requirements for Pharmaceuticals for Human Use (ICH) guidelines, and Indian guidelines, including those provided by the Indian Council of Medical Research (ICMR).

The protocol components discussed include study objectives, study design, study population and eligibility criteria, outcome measures, sample size calculation, ethical considerations and informed consent. Furthermore, the write-up emphasizes the importance of addressing adverse events and their management, study monitoring and supervision, study assessments, study conduct, investigational product management, and the inclusion of essential appendices such as the informed consent form, patient information sheet, and case record form.

Writing a protocol poses challenges such as formulating clear study objectives, selecting appropriate study designs, defining eligibility criteria, selecting culturally sensitive outcome measures, accurately calculating sample sizes, and ensuring ethical considerations and informed consent. Researchers must also address adverse event management, study monitoring, and supervision to ensure data quality and participant safety. Additionally, incorporating appropriate study assessments, study conduct guidelines, and investigational product management procedures are crucial for the successful implementation of clinical trials.

By addressing these challenges and incorporating robust protocol components, researchers can design rigorous clinical trials that contribute to scientific knowledge, improve patient care, and adhere to both international and Indian guidelines.

Introduction

Clinical trials play a crucial role in advancing medical knowledge and facilitating the development of new treatments and interventions. The design of a clinical trial is a meticulous process that involves various protocol components. However, researchers often encounter challenges when writing a protocol. This write-up provides an overview of the key protocol components and highlights commonly faced during protocol development in clinical trials.

What is a Clinical Trial Protocol?

Clinical trial protocols are documents that describe the objectives, design, methodology, statistical considerations and aspects related to the organization of clinical trials. They provide the background and rationale for conducting a study, highlighting specific research questions

Corresponding author: Dr Suyog Sindhu. Can be contacted at phone number+91 91981 69265.
Email id: suyog@kgmcindia.edu

that are addressed, and taking into consideration ethical issues. These must meet a standard that adheres to the principles of Good Clinical Practice, and are used to obtain ethics approval by local Ethics Committees or Institutional Review Boards.

Study Objectives:

Defining clear and relevant study objectives is crucial but can be challenging in both the international and Indian scenarios. Researchers may encounter difficulties in aligning the study objectives with the specific healthcare needs, cultural considerations, and disease burden prevalent in each context. Balancing international scientific standards, such as the International Council for Harmonisation of Technical Requirements for Pharmaceuticals for Human Use (ICH) guidelines, with local health challenges requires careful consideration and incorporation of both international and Indian perspectives.

Study Design:

Selecting an appropriate study design is essential but can be influenced by factors specific to each context. Researchers may face challenges in determining the optimal design considering local disease patterns, resource constraints, patient preferences, and cultural factors. Balancing ethical considerations, such as equitable access to interventions, with the need for rigorous scientific evidence can pose challenges during protocol development. Adhering to both international guidelines, such as the ICH guidelines, and Indian guidelines, such as those provided by the Indian Council of Medical Research (ICMR), ensures compliance with global standards while addressing local considerations.

Study Population and Eligibility Criteria:

Defining the study population and eligibility criteria can be complex in both international and Indian contexts due to diverse demographics, cultural variations, and healthcare disparities.

Researchers need to carefully consider representation across different regions, socioeconomic backgrounds, and healthcare settings to ensure the trial's generalizability. Striking a balance between inclusivity and homogeneity is crucial for obtaining valid results and ensuring equitable access to study participation. Incorporating both international and Indian guidelines helps ensure appropriate participant selection and diversity while addressing ethical considerations specific to each context.

Outcome Measures:

Selecting appropriate outcome measures can be challenging in both the international and Indian scenarios. Researchers must consider cultural and contextual factors that may influence the interpretation and relevance of outcome measures. Incorporating patient-reported outcomes, cultural-specific endpoints, and measures that capture the impact of the intervention on local healthcare needs is essential. Collaboration with local experts, patient advocacy groups, and considering international guidelines, such as the ICH guidelines, can assist in selecting culturally sensitive and meaningful outcome measures.

Sample Size Calculation:

Accurate sample size calculation is vital for the statistical power and validity of clinical trials conducted both internationally and in India. However, estimating effect sizes, dropout rates, and accounting for local variations in disease prevalence and treatment response can present challenges. Researchers should consult with biostatisticians familiar with the specific context and leverage existing data or pilot studies to inform sample size calculations. Incorporating both international guidelines, such as the ICH guidelines, and local considerations ensures appropriate sample size determination and statistical power.

Ethical Considerations and Informed Consent:

Addressing ethical considerations and obtaining informed consent are paramount in both international and Indian scenarios. Researchers must adhere to both international ethical guidelines, such as the ICH guideline for Good Clinical Practice (GCP), and local guidelines, such as those provided by the ICMR in India. Sensitivity to cultural norms, language barriers, and literacy levels is crucial during the informed consent process. Researchers should ensure that informed consent forms are clear, comprehensible, and culturally appropriate, enabling participants to make informed decisions while complying with both international and local guidelines.

Adverse Events and their Management:

Protocol development should include plans for monitoring and managing adverse events. Researchers need to define adverse event reporting procedures, including the documentation, assessment, and reporting of adverse events during the trial. Incorporating guidelines from regulatory bodies, such as the ICH guidelines for safety reporting, and local regulatory requirements ensures comprehensive adverse event management.

Study Monitoring and Supervision:

Adequate study monitoring and supervision are critical for ensuring the quality and integrity of clinical trials. Researchers should develop a comprehensive plan for study monitoring, including data monitoring, site visits, and oversight of trial conduct. Incorporating international guidelines, such as the ICH guidelines for good clinical practice, and local requirements helps ensure effective study monitoring and adherence to ethical and regulatory standards.

Study Assessments:

Protocol development should include a clear description of study assessments to be performed during the trial. This includes specifying the schedule, methods, and tools for data collection, clinical examinations, laboratory tests, imaging studies, and other evaluations as appropriate.

Incorporating standardized assessment tools, such as those recommended by international guidelines and validated measures specific to the Indian context, ensures consistency and accuracy in data collection.

Study Conduct and Treatment:

Clearly defining study conduct procedures is crucial for ensuring consistency and adherence to the protocol. This includes detailing treatment administration, intervention protocols, follow-up schedules, and procedures for data collection and documentation. Researchers should consider international guidelines, such as the ICH guidelines, as well as local treatment practices and standards of care in India.

Investigational Product Management:

If the trial involves investigational products, comprehensive guidelines for their management should be included in the protocol. This includes procedures for procurement, storage, labeling, dispensing, and accountability of investigational products. Adhering to both international guidelines, such as the ICH guidelines on investigational product management, and Indian regulatory requirements ensures appropriate handling and documentation of investigational products.

Appendices:

Protocol development should include essential appendices, such as the informed consent form, patient information sheet, and case record form. The informed consent form should adhere to both international and Indian guidelines, providing clear and comprehensive information to participants. The patient information sheet should be culturally appropriate and provide accessible information about the trial in a language and format understandable to participants. The case record form should be carefully designed to capture all relevant data points and adhere to both international guidelines, such as the ICH guidelines for case report form design, and local requirements.

Conclusion

Developing clinical trial protocols in the international and Indian contexts requires navigating challenges specific to each setting while adhering to international standards. Incorporating both international guidelines, such as the ICH guidelines, and Indian guidelines, such as those provided by the ICMR, helps researchers design comprehensive protocols that generate reliable evidence, address local health challenges, and contribute to improving healthcare outcomes globally and in India.

References:

1. Cipriani A, Barbui C. What is a clinical trial protocol? Epidemiol Psichiatr Soc. 2010 Apr-Jun;19(2):116-7. PMID: 20815294.

2. International Council for Harmonisation of Technical Requirements for Pharmaceuticals for Human Use (ICH). ICH Harmonised Guideline: Integrated Addendum to ICH E6 (R1): Guideline for Good Clinical Practice E6 (R2). 2016. Available at: https://database.ich.org/sites/default/files/E6_R2_Addendum.pdf. (Accessed: 10th July 2023.)

3. Indian Council of Medical Research (ICMR). Ethical Guidelines for Biomedical Research on Human Participants. 2017. Available at: https://www.icmr.gov.in/ethical_guidelines.pdf. (Accessed: 10th July 2023).

4. Indian Council of Medical Research (ICMR). National Ethical Guidelines for Biomedical and Health Research Involving Human Participants. 2017. Available at: www.icmr.gov.in/guidelines/ICMR_Ethical_Guidelines_2017.pdf. (Accessed: 10th July 2023).

5. Chow SC, Liu JP. Design and Analysis of Clinical Trials: Concepts and Methodologies. 3rd edition. John Wiley & Sons, 2014. ISBN: 978-0470-45426-7.

6. Pocock SJ, et al. Clinical Trials: A Practical Approach. John Wiley & Sons, 2019. ISBN: 978-111-938-986-6.

Chapter 06

CDSCO and its current Procedures for Clinical Trial Approval in India

Mr. Anirudh Sahoo, M Pharm.
Senior Project Manager, George Clinical, Bangalore, India.

Abstract

Without CDSCO approval, no clinical trials can be initiated in India. Documents required for submission, review and approval of CT application is well defined. The Schedule Y of the Drugs and Cosmetics Act (DCA) and Rules there under specify requirements for clinical trials and market authorization. The reviews of applications for granting authorization to conduct clinical trials or to market a new drug in the country, require a multidisciplinary assessment by regulatory authorities (RAs) and scientific experts, to ensure that the applications meet the necessary regulatory standards and scientific evidence for safety, efficacy and quality. Good review practices assist the RAs to achieve timely and quality review. A complete application is a prerequisite to ensure an efficient review process. In this article documents required for CT application and the processes involved in successful approval of the same is discussed.

Objective

To understand the submission of application and the procedure to get Clinical trial permission to conduct the study. The Schedule Y of the Drugs and Cosmetics Act (DCA) and Rules there under specify requirements for clinical trials and market authorization.

The reviews of applications for granting authorization to conduct clinical trials or to market a new drug in the country, require a multidisciplinary assessment by regulatory authorities (RAs) and scientific experts, to ensure that the applications meet the necessary regulatory standards and scientific evidence for safety, efficacy and quality. Good review practices assist the RAs to achieve timely and quality review. A complete application is a prerequisite to ensure an efficient review process.

How it is applicable to day today CT operation

In accordance with the 2019-CTRules, the sponsor (also known as the applicant) is required to submit a clinical trial application to the Drugs Controller General of India (DCGI),), to obtain authorization to conduct a clinical trial in India. (Note: The DCGI is commonly referred to as the Central Licensing Authority in the Indian regulations.) The investigator must also obtain ethics committee (EC) approval from a DCGI-registered EC prior to initiating a study.

As indicated in the Notice:15Jan18, all clinical trial application submissions must be submitted electronically via CDSCO's SUGAM portal (IND-59) (Link: CDSCO (cdscoonline.gov.in).

Types of Submissions
Applications could be for
- Investigational New Drug Clinical Trials
- New Drugs Clinical Trials (Local bridging clinical trials of drugs already approved outside for obtaining marketing authorization i.e. permission for import/manufacture for sale in India)
- Global Clinical Trials (clinical trials in various phases of development as a part of multinational clinical development)
- Post Marketing Studies

Corresponding author: Mr. Anirudh Sahoo. Can be contacted at phone number+91 91605 04681
Email id: anirudhsahoo@gmail.com

Regulatory Authority Requirements for submission:

As per the 2019-CTRules, documentation must be submitted to the Drugs Controller General of India (DCGI), head of the Central Drugs Standard Control Organization (CDSCO), as part of the approval process for investigational new drugs (INDs) will depend upon the type of application, phase of the study, stage in drug development process, and/or objective of the study. Information that may be required is included in the lists below (Note: The regulatory sources provide overlapping and unique elements so each of the items listed above will not necessarily be in each source):

- Form CT-04 (the clinical trial application form including sponsor (also known as applicant) name; sponsor nature/constitution and contact information; clinical trials site contact information and details; contact information for person responsible for compensation payment, if any; correspondence address; new drug/investigational new drug name(s) and details (i.e., therapeutic class, dosage form, composition, and indications); clinical trial phase; protocol number with date; and ethics committee (EC) and investigator names)
- Treasury Challan receipt demonstrating payment of corresponding fee or transaction ID
- Chemical and pharmaceutical information
- Animal pharmacology data
- Animal toxicology data
- Human clinical pharmacology data
- Active ingredient information (for INDs and global clinical trials (GCTs))
- Formulation data (for INDs and GCTs)
- Therapeutic class (for INDs and GCTs)
- Regulatory status in India and in other countries
- Proposed study status in other participating countries and any approvals, withdrawals, discontinuation of approval, etc. (for GCTs)
- Affidavit stating study has not been discontinued in any country (for GCTs)
- Prescribing information
- Testing protocol(s) for quality control testing
- Relevance of study, investigational drug, or any specific study aspects to the health care needs of India.

- Innovation vis-à-vis existing therapeutic options
- Unmet medical need in the country (as applicable)
- Any India-specific safety/dosage concerns/ investigational tests to be done
- Clinical study reports should be submitted per the International Conference on Harmonisation (ICH) Common Technical Document (CTD) (IND-68)
- Protocol safety measures per toxicological studies; early clinical studies, approved product insert for marketed product, and published literature
- Investigator's Brochure (IB)
- Investigational Medicinal Products Dossier (IMPD) (for (GCTs))
- Affidavit stating the IB information is correct and based on facts (for GCTs)
- Source of bulk drugs (for INDs)
- Treasury Challan with Form CT-16 (import license application) (for GCTs)
- Sponsor authorization letter (for GCTs)
- Details of biological specimens to be exported and the online application for export no objection certificate (NOC) for biological samples on the SUGAM portal (IND-59) (for GCTs) (See IND-1 for the application form to request a NOC to export biological samples) (Refer to the Specimens topic for more information on specimen import/export)
- Case Report Form (CRF)
- Informed consent form (ICF) and patient information sheet (See Required Elements section for additional information)
- Investigator(s) undertaking
- EC approvals (if available)
- Clinical study report(s)
- Investigator list in India and site address

Refer to the 2019-CTRules and IND-31 to obtain detailed submission requirements for applications to conduct a clinical trial using an already approved new drug with a new indication, a new dosage form/new route of administration, a modified release dosage form, or a new drug with an additional strength.

Reviews

<u>Reviews By DCGI</u>
    Regulatory aspects
    Administrative procedures

<u>By Subject Expert</u>
    Preclinical, toxicological, clinical data submitted
    Proposed clinical trial/ marketing approval

Focus of SEC Review:
    Risk vs. benefit
    Innovation vs. existing therapy
    Unmet medical need
    Ethical aspects for patient safety
    India specific concerns

Flow chart of the Import & Registration Regulatory process:

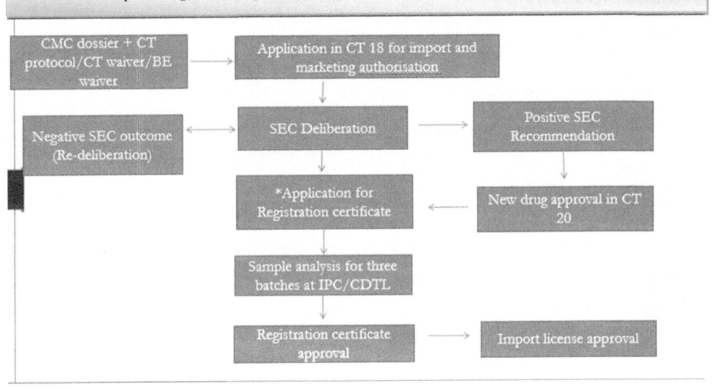

Flow chart of Regulatory process for Indigenous Product:

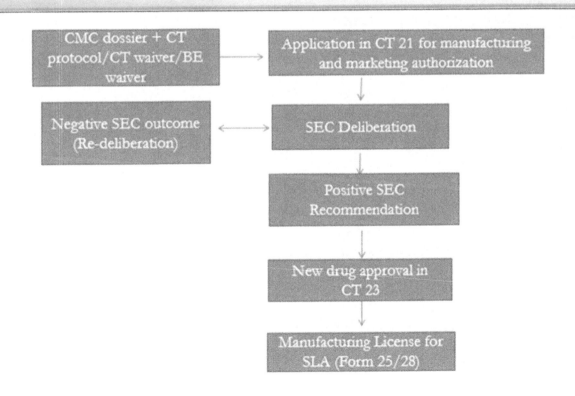

Common problems seen in day-to-day implementation:

- Site selection and engagement (50/50 distribution of site between Govt. and Pvt. Hospitals/Institutions).
- Quality management
- Trial data management (Inconsistent internet connectivity at a few sites and lack of option of offline data entry in the database platform used in the trial)
- Institution/Site documentation viz update CV of PI, MRC and GCP certificates
- Clinical trial approval and delays
- Delay in ethical clearance
- Clinical late phase trial CRO to be registered (Clarity underway from CDSCO)

How to adopt/Overcome the challenges:

- Robust infrastructure at Govt site level (Implement a specific Clinical trial department and function as in Pvt organization with the help of CRO (Contract Research Organization) Or SMO (Site Management Organization).
- An independent quality team to ensure the processes by developing and implementing the SOPs.
- Good documentation practice while collecting the Site documents
- Robust infrastructure (High speed internet with power backup systems
- Deployment of Qualified personnel with proper training
- Robust Study Design
- Approval processes by faster re-deliberation of protocol by SEC

Conclusion:

Indian regulatory system (CDSCO) has remarkably improved in the arena of Clinical study approval systems by adopting online systems. In recent past there are many changes happened which favors the global clinical trials to be conducted in India. However there many things still need improvement to conduct the clinical studies as per GCP.

References
1. CDSCO's SUGAM portal
2. Handbook for Applicants And Reviewers Of Clinical Trials Of New Drugs In India
3. NDCT Rule2019

Chapter 07

Good Statistical Practice in Clinical Trial

Dr Gayathri Vishwakarma
MSc, PhD (in Statistics), MBA (Quality Management),
Lead Biostatistician, George Institute for Global Health,
New Delhi.

Abstract

Statistical expertise is crucial in the planning, execution, and analysis of clinical trials. It ensures that the study is properly designed, the data is appropriately analyzed, and the results are valid and reliable. Proper statistical methods help researchers make accurate inferences and draw meaningful conclusions from clinical trial data.

More serious are errors due to negligence. Innumerable deaths occur due to wrong conclusion arrived by inappropriate analysis and inaccurate data and several times, these go unnoticed. These errors can be minimized, by adhering the GCP guidelines. This article discusses the statistical points to be considered at the time of planning, executing and summarizing the results of a clinical trial.

Background

Statistics plays a vital role in the design, analysis, and interpretation of data in clinical trials. Statistical errors can cause many deaths[1] or misinterpretation of research findings. Wrong results even by just one per cent and adopted for practice on millions of patients, can compromise health and life of thousands of people. Substandard research can make vulnerable many lives.

Reducing statistical errors in clinical trials is crucial for ensuring the validity and reliability of study findings. Key strategies need to be followed to reduce statistical errors such as proper study design, robust statistical analysis plan, rigorous data collection and quality control, minimizing missing data, statistical expertise, independent statistical review and transparency and reproducibility.

What can be done to reduce statistical errors?

By implementing these strategies, researchers can minimize statistical errors and enhance the quality and reliability of the findings from clinical trials. Collaboration with experienced statisticians and Good statistical practice is the key for clinical research which guides on ethical and scientific framework.[2] part of the trial and

ICH GCP E6 guideline emphasizes on two points i.e. an experienced statistician has be to adherence to established guidelines, such as ICH-Good Clinical Practice (GCP) and CDSCO Indian GCP, are also essential for reducing statistical errors. statistical analysis plan should be clear, concise, and operationally feasible.[3]

In India, GCP guidelines and Schedule Y has been followed for years in conducting clinical trials. Now guidelines are updated and section 2.3.1.9 talks about statistics.[4] Central Drugs Standard Control Organization released GCP inspection checklist for global trials.[5] The guidelines stressed on two cardinal principles: protection of the rights of human subjects and authenticity of biomedical data generated. Table 1 explains the key aspects of statistics discussed in Indian GCP.

Sample size is a crucial aspect of clinical trials and plays a significant role in the validity and reliability of the study results. The importance of sample size in clinical trials can be understood through statistical Power. Insufficient sample size can lead to low power, resulting in a higher likelihood of false-negative findings (Type II errors) and failure to detect true treatment effects. A sample size that is representative and sufficiently large enhances the generalizability of study findings to the target population.

Corresponding author: Dr Gayathri Vishwakarma. Can be contacted at phone number +91 95558 61313.
Email id: gayatri.singh.v@gmail.com

Table 1: Key aspects of statistics in CDSCO GCP and ICH GCP

Statistical Concept	Justification	
	CDSCO GCP	ICH GCP
Sample Size Determination	Emphasis is on the importance of appropriate sample size determination. Based on the study objectives, expected effect size, variability, and significance level.	Emphasizes the importance of appropriate sample size determination as adequate sample size helps ensure that the study has sufficient power to detect meaningful treatment effects and draw valid conclusions.
Randomization and Treatment Allocation	Randomization methods are used to assign participants to different treatment groups in a clinical trial. It put emphasis on describing proper randomization techniques to ensure that the treatment groups are comparable and minimize selection bias.	Research requires proper randomization techniques to ensure that the treatment groups are comparable and minimize selection bias. This includes methods such as simple randomization, stratified randomization, and block randomization.
Statistical Analysis Plan (SAP)	Mentions the importance of a pre-specified SAP. The SAP outlines the statistical methods that will be used to analyze the data collected during the clinical trial. It includes details on the primary and secondary endpoints, statistical tests, subgroup analyses, and handling of missing data.	ICH GCP emphasizes the importance of a pre-specified SAP. It includes details on the primary and secondary endpoints, statistical tests, subgroup analyses, handling of missing data, and any planned interim analyses. The SAP should be developed and finalized before the database is locked to ensure transparency and prevent post hoc analysis.
Data Monitoring and Quality Control	Ongoing data monitoring and quality control procedures throughout the clinical trial is must. Appropriate statistical method should be used to assess the data quality.	Underline the need for ongoing data monitoring and quality control procedures throughout the clinical trial. These procedures involve regular monitoring of data collection, data validation checks, identification, and resolution of data discrepancies, and ensuring data integrity. Statistical methods should be used to detect outliers, assess data quality, and ensure accurate and reliable trial data.
Statistical Analysis	This section highlights the importance of appropriate statistical analysis of clinical trial data. Statistical methods are used to analyze primary and secondary endpoints, safety data, and other relevant outcomes. The analysis should adhere to the pre-specified SAP to ensure transparency and reproducibility.	The analysis should be conducted according to the pre-specified SAP and statistical principles to ensure robust and reliable results. Statistical methods must be mentioned beforehand for proposed mock tables, listing and figures. Statistical methods such as hypothesis testing, confidence interval estimation, survival analysis, regression analysis, and subgroup analysis are used to analyze primary and secondary endpoints, safety data, and other relevant outcomes.
Reporting of Results	There is a requirement of clear and accurate reporting of the statistical analysis results. The results should be presented in a manner that is understandable and interpretable.	Results should be understandable and interpretable including proper use of central tendency, variability, statistical significance, effect sizes, and confidence intervals. The reporting should follow the ICH guidelines for Clinical Study Reports (CSRs) to ensure consistency and transparency.
Independent Statistical Review (ISR)	It advocates an independent statistical review of the study design, SAP, and statistical analysis conducted for the clinical trial. This review confirms that the statistical methods used are appropriate and adhere to GCP guidelines.	ICH GCP may recommend an independent statistical review of the study design, SAP, and statistical analysis conducted for the clinical trial. This review ensures that the statistical methods used are appropriate, unbiased, and adhere to ICH GCP principles.

A larger sample size helps ensure that the study population is diverse enough to capture the characteristics of the target population, improving the external validity of the study. Adequate sample size is necessary to ensure ethical considerations in clinical trials.

Conducting a study with an insufficient sample size may expose participants to potential risks without providing them with the opportunity to contribute to meaningful scientific knowledge. Sample size estimation also takes into account practical factors, such as cost and availability of resources such as funding, personnel, infrastructure, and participant recruitment efforts. Determining an appropriate sample size allows for efficient utilization of resources and ensures that the study is feasible within the available constraints.

Randomization is a fundamental principle in clinical trials and holds great importance in ensuring the validity and reliability of study results. It helps minimize selection bias, which occurs when certain characteristics or factors influence the assignment of participants to treatment groups. This reduces the potential for confounding variables and ensures that any observed differences in outcomes between groups can be attributed to the treatments being compared rather than other factors. It creates comparable treatment groups and balance factors which helps ensure that any differences in outcomes are more likely to be due to the treatment being investigated rather than differences in participant characteristics. Randomization thus strengthens the internal validity of the study. Randomization helps control for unknown or unmeasured factors that may influence treatment outcomes. By randomly assigning participants, any unknown factors that could potentially affect treatment response are likely to be distributed equally among the groups, minimizing their impact on the study results.

CRF (Case Report Form) development and data capturing are crucial components of clinical trials. CRFs are structured documents used to collect and record data during a clinical trial. The development of CRFs begins with the study protocol.

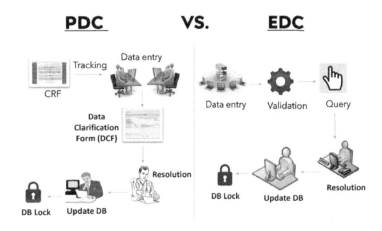

The protocol outlines the objectives, design, procedures, and endpoints of the clinical trial. It serves as a foundation for determining the data elements to be collected. A data dictionary is created to define and describe each data element to be collected on the CRFs. This includes specifying the variable name, data type, format, and any coding or validation rules. Based on the study protocol and data dictionary, the CRFs are designed. The CRFs should be clear, concise, and capture all the necessary information required for the study. The format and layout of the CRFs should be user-friendly and facilitate accurate and efficient data entry. In addition to paper-based data capture (PDC), electronic data capture (EDC) systems are increasingly used in clinical trials. EDC systems allow for direct data entry into a secure database, reducing errors and enabling real-time data monitoring. EDC systems may involve interactive CRFs, data entry screens, and automated data checks. Before data collection begins, training sessions need to be conducted for investigators, study coordinators, and site personnel involved in data collection. The training covers the CRF completion guidelines, data entry procedures, and any specific instructions related to data capturing. Once the study is initiated, the data collection process begins. Study participants' information is recorded on the CRFs either in paper format or through the EDC system. Throughout the trial, data monitoring and quality control procedures are implemented to ensure data accuracy and integrity. This may involve regular monitoring visits, source data verification, and data validation checks. Any discrepancies or errors in the data are identified and resolved.

After the completion of data collection, a thorough data cleaning process is conducted to identify and rectify any data inconsistencies or errors.

Once the data has been cleaned and validated, the database is locked, preventing further modifications to the data. Following database lock, the collected data is analyzed using appropriate statistical methods as outlined in the statistical analysis plan. The results of the analysis contribute to the study findings and support decision-making.

Throughout the entire process of CRF development and data capturing, regulatory requirements and guidelines must be adhered to. This includes compliance with Good Clinical Practice (GCP) guidelines, data privacy and protection regulations, and any specific regulations imposed by regulatory authorities. Effective CRF development and accurate data capturing are crucial for ensuring the reliability and validity of clinical trial results. A well-designed CRF and a robust data capture process contribute to the integrity of the study and support evidence-based conclusions.

Blinding and concealment are important methodological techniques used in clinical trials to minimize bias and enhance the validity of study results. They serve different purposes and are implemented to ensure the integrity of the research.

Blinding involves suppressing information about treatment assignment from one or more par

ties involved in the study. Blinding can be employed in different ways: a. Single-Blind: Participants are unaware of their treatment assignment, while researchers and/or outcome assessors are aware. b. Double-Blind: Both participants and researchers/outcome assessors are unaware of the treatment assignment. c. Triple-Blind: In addition to participants and researchers/outcome assessors, data analysts or statisticians analyzing the results are also unaware of the treatment assignment.

Concealment describes to the process of protecting the randomization sequence and concealing the treatment allocation until the point of intervention assignment. It ensures that the treatment assignment remains unknown to those involved in participant recruitment and enrollment.

By integrating blinding and concealment in clinical trials, one can achieve Internal Validity Strengthens Credibility, Supports Comparability and meets Ethical Considerations.

Clinical data management tools play a crucial role in the collection, organization, storage, and analysis of data in clinical trials. These tools facilitate efficient and accurate data management throughout the entire research process.

The commonly used clinical data management tools in clinical trials are Electronic Data Capture (EDC) Systems, Clinical Trial Management System (CTMS), Electronic Patient Reported Outcome (ePRO) Tools, Randomization and

Table 2: Blinding and concealment

Importance	
Blinding	**Concealment**
Blinding helps prevent conscious or subconscious biases that can arise from knowledge of treatment assignment. It reduces the potential for differential treatment, assessment, and reporting of outcomes between the intervention and control groups.	Concealment of treatment allocation ensures that participants and researchers involved in recruitment cannot predict or influence the group to which participants will be assigned. This helps prevent selection bias, which can occur when participants are non-randomly assigned to groups based on known or unknown factors.
Blinding boosts objectivity in data collection, analysis, and interpretation. It reduces the influence of subjective factors and personal beliefs on the study outcomes.	Concealment maintains the integrity of the randomization process, ensuring that treatment groups are balanced and comparable. It helps guarantee that the treatment assignment is not influenced by external factors or preferences.
Blinding can help control for placebo effects by ensuring that participants and outcome assessors are unaware of the treatment assignment. This is particularly relevant when studying subjective outcomes or interventions with strong psychological or subjective components.	

Trial Supply Management (RTSM) Systems, and Clinical Data Management Systems (CDMS).

These clinical data management tools streamline data collection, ensure data integrity, and support efficient data analysis. The selection of appropriate data management tools depends on the specific requirements of the trial, budget considerations, and regulatory compliance.

Statistical Software: Several statistical analysis software packages, such as SAS, R, or STATA, are commonly used in clinical trials for data analysis. These tools enable researchers to conduct statistical analyses, generate summary reports, and interpret study results.

Conclusion

Errors become more serious because of negligence. Many statisticians and medical professionals equally neglect to make a distinction between statistical significance and medical significance. Statistical inference heavily depends on sample size. Entire team involved in clinical trial must be GCP trained with the same rigorousness as it is done for investigators/clinicians.

Conflict interest: none declared.

Acknowledgement: none declared.

References:

1. Indrayan A. Statistical fallacies & errors can also jeopardize life & health of many. Indian J Med Res 148, December 2018, pp 677-679 DOI: 10.4103/ijmr.IJMR_853_18
2. Good statistical toolkit by OECD council. 2021 Available from: https://www.oecd.org/statistics/good-practice-toolkit/
3. ICH E6-R3 GCP-Principles: Explanatory Note. 2021. Available from: https://database.ich.org/sites/default/files/ICH_E6-R3_GCP-Principles_Draft_2021_0419.pdf
4. Central Drugs Standard Control Organization (CDSCO) GCP. Available from: https://cdsco.gov.in/opencms/opencms/system/modules/CDSCO.WEB/elements/download_file_division.jsp?num_id=MzM5NQ==
5. GCP INSPECTION CHECKLIST. CDSCO. 2023. https://cdsco.gov.in/opencms/opencms/system/modules/CDSCO.WEB/elements/download_file_division.jsp?num_id=NTI=

Chapter 08

Principles of Ethics in Clinical Research and Ethics Committee Composition

Dr Sapna Patil MBBS MD
PGDMLE, CCEBDM, PDCR,PCPV and GCP,
PGDMLE from National Law School, Bangalore, CCEBDM from PHFI,
Associate Professor, Department of Pharmacology,
Sapthagiri institute of medical sciences and research center,
Bengaluru , Karnataka.

Abstract

Clinical research is designed to improve human health and increase our understanding of human biology, ultimately leading to significant advances in scientific knowledge. The number of registered clinical trials has increased drastically in recent years, and these studies are crucial for researching and developing novel drugs for treatment purposes. A host of legal issues arise during the conduct of clinical research, like adequate consent on the part of test subjects, liabilities of the researchers if the test subject is harmed, or any form of research that needs to be considered illegal on ethical grounds, but still, the law itself demands the conduct of clinical research before drugs are introduced into the market.

There are numerous national as well as international guidelines for the conduct of clinical trials. **Ethics** is the branch of philosophy that takes a systematic approach to defining *social* and *individual* **morality**—the fundamental standards of right and wrong that a whole society, as well as individuals, learn from their culture and peers.

Introduction

The progress of medical knowledge and therapeutic medicine is impossible without research in medicine and therapy. Clinical research is designed to improve human health and increase our understanding of human biology, ultimately leading to significant advances in scientific knowledge.

The number of registered clinical trials has increased drastically in recent years, and these studies are crucial for researching and developing novel drugs for treatment purposes. Such new medicines that are developed by scientists have to be tested for their safety, therapeutic value, and effectiveness (efficacy) before they are made available for prescription by doctors.

For this, initially animal studies have to be conducted, but such studies may not give a complete picture of the effects of these new compounds on human beings. Research on human beings is like a necessary evil that humanity needs to negotiate with to achieve progress in therapeutics and safer modalities for disease treatment. There are two competing interests, both of which are of immense social value. The need to improve therapeutic compounds, which can save lives, and the need to respect and preserve the dignity and safety of individuals participating in clinical trials

Hence, a host of legal issues arise during the conduct of clinical research, like adequate consent on the part of test subjects, liabilities of the researchers if the

Corresponding author: Dr Sapna Patil. Can be contacted at phone number+91 98456 15021.
Email id: sapnapatil75@gmail.com

test subject is harmed, and any forms of research that need to be considered illegal on ethical grounds, but still, the law itself demands the conduct of clinical research before drugs are introduced into the market.

Why are regulations and codes of ethics important in clinical research?

Regulatory and ethical principles have been put in place over the years due to unfortunate cases of unethical research that have occurred throughout history. One of the most well-known cases is the Tuskegee Syphilis Study. This unethical trial involved the deceptive administration of placebos to 400 African American males in Alabama with syphilis. These participants were made to believe that they were receiving treatment when researchers never intended to give any treatment but instead performed the trial to assess the progression of syphilis over time.

It is always difficult to make a clear distinction between treatment and research. Most trials are conducted under conditions of a certain degree of uncertainty, and doctors tend to learn continuously from the outcomes of their patients' treatments.

Regulation Of Clinical Research

The International Ethical Guidelines

1. **The Nürnberg Code of 1946:** includes 10 principles to guide physician-investigators in experiments involving human subjects, especially the first principle on "voluntary consent". This was based on the medical code of ethics at the time of Nazi atrocities, which did not address the consent of human subjects.
2. **The Thalidomide Disaster of 1962:** While Thalidomide was being studied for use in the US, it was discovered that the drug caused

congenital malformation in the foetus (phcomelia) when taken by pregnant women during the first trimester of pregnancy.

3. Declaration OF Helsinki, 1964: A statement of ethical principles to provide guidance to doctors and other participants involved in clinical research The International Code of Medical Ethics declares that "a physician shall act only in the patient's interest when providing medical care that might have the effect of weakening the physical and mental condition of the patient" .

3. ICH-GCP of 1997: The FDA has published guidelines entitled "Good Clinical Practice under the auspices of the International Conference on Harmonisation of Technical Requirements of Pharmaceuticals for Human Use (ICH). The objective is to provide a unified standard to facilitate the mutual acceptance of clinical trial data by the regulatory authorities.

GCP Guidelines for Conducting Clinical Research in India

1. ICH-GCP guidelines, 1997: The guidelines should be followed when generating clinical research data that are intended to be submitted to regulatory authorities.
2. Ethical Guidelines for Biomedical Research on Human Subjects, 2006, ICMR Code: The Indian Council of Medical Research, New Delhi, issued the ICMR Code in 2000; the revised guidelines were released in 2006. The guidelines are applicable for the clinical evaluation of drugs, vaccines, devices, diagnostics, herbal remedies, etc.

3. GCP, 2001 (Indian GCP): The Drug Technical Advisory Board, the highest body under the Drugs and Cosmetics Act 1940 and Rules 1945, has endorsed adoption of the GCP guidelines for the conduct of clinical trials in India.

3. Schedule Y, Amended Version, 2005: It details the rules for the conduct of clinical trials in India. The Schedule also elaborates on each phase of the clinical trial, the nature of the phase, the information to be collected, and the precautions to be maintained in each phase.

Principles Relating to Clinical Research Ethics:

1. **Value or social value:** The simplest way of understanding it is to ask whether this research question has any value either socially, scientifically, or clinically, and whether it's worth answering.

2. **Validity:** Once an IRB has established that the research has value, the next question is whether the proposed study has an acceptable scientific design, statistical methodology, implementation strategy, and feasibility so that the research question can be answered. For example, in the 1990s, there was a great deal of discussion about the effectiveness of giving antiretroviral treatment to health care workers who had been accidentally pricked with a needle that might have been contaminated with HIV. Post-exposure prophylaxis was the term used for this type of treatment.

"It's an important question to answer, but the design of such a study seemed impossible because the incidence of transmission was so low that an enormous number of people were required to answer the question. So a randomised control trial was never conducted, and instead public health officials relied on data from case reports.

3. **Fair subject selection:** This is basically the notion that people should be selected to participate based on a scientific question and not for other reasons, such as favour or disfavour or ease of manipulation. Once scientifically appropriate participants are identified, there still needs to be consideration of vulnerability, risk, and benefit, and so you balance the need to fairly select people with the need to minimise risks with the people who are selected.

There should be an equitable selection of subjects, with special attention paid to vulnerable and high risk subjects. There must be evidence of an unbiased selection of subjects reflected in the periodic review and must be as per the inclusion and exclusion criteria of the study protocol.

4. **Risk/benefit:** This principle is more complicated than its label. The subjects should be informed and will have to comprehend the associated risks and benefits of the trial.

The notion is that even after obtaining a valuable question, a rigorous design that will answer it, a fair subject selection process, and a goal, there is still more that can be done to minimise risk and maximise benefits for the participants in this study.

Independent review: While this is a procedural requirement, it has other benefits, such as public accountability, It's a way to check both enthusiasm and potential conflicts on the part of investigators. Enthusiasm without careful methodology could lead one to their own conclusions.

So an independent review of the proposal, methodology, and statistical analysis plan serves to check that kind of enthusiasm that could lead to the wrong conclusion. IRBs worked most effectively for smaller, institutional research, but the complexity of today's multi-site and multi-national research has raised questions about whether the current system is correct.

6.**Informed consent:** "If you don't justify the risks and benefits, then you never ask people to participate, so while informed consent is an important part of doing research and a universal requirement, it's not where you start."
Informed consent is based on people's ability to make their own decisions, and they need the right amount of information to make this decision.

The informed consent processes must be reviewed by the Ethics committee to ensure that the subject or impartial witness is provided with appropriate information and adequate time.

7.**Respect for enrolled participants:** This category reflects the notion that even after you have carefully designed a study and individuals have consented to participate voluntarily, there are still things one needs to do to show respect for the individuals who have chosen to participate. It includes monitoring the well-being of the individuals in the study, protecting their confidentiality, making relevant information available that people would need to know to make a relevant decision about continuing participation, and reminding them that they have the right to withdraw from the study if they want to.
An infamous example of research that lacked ethical respect for participants was the Tuskegee study, in which African American men were enrolled as part of a study of the symptoms of syphilis.

When the study began, antibiotics were not a proven treatment for syphilis, but as participation in the study continued over decades, the research participants had the right to receive antibiotic treatment but were not informed of its availability.

8.**Confidentiality and privacy of the subjects:** This shall be maintained.

9.**Compensation provided to subjects for participation:** Compensation must be paid to the subjects as per the informed consent document, contract, and applicable rules and regulations. This amount must be approved by the Ethics committee.

10.**Serious Adverse Events must be addressed:** Adequate medical care is provided for SAE as per the applicable rules and regulations. SAE reporting timelines and compensation should be as per the regulation.

Compensation for injury to the subject should be as per the rules and regulations and monitored for non-compliance.

11. Protection of subject rights, safety, and wellbeing: If the need arises, complaints and concerns of subjects shall be addressed and managed appropriately. The Ethics committee must have a "Subject Grievance Redressal" process. Subjects should be contacted randomly, and interviewed during visits.

12. Adequate finance, human resource allocation for administrative work, and record keeping must be ensured with care and confidentiality. There must be financial transparency in the functioning of the ethics committee.

13. Proposals involving special populations, pregnant mothers and children, and **vulnerable subjects** should be evaluated as per rules and regulations.

14. Conflict of Interest Policy: This shall be declared, prior to the review and voluntary withdrawal during the decision-making process.

15. Security, confidentiality, and integrity of documents: Systematic record keeping of all documents must be present.

Documents and records shall be **archived** after trial completion or termination as per applicable rules and regulations.

16. Autonomy: The **subject or patient** has freedom of thought, intention, and action when making decisions regarding health care procedures For a patient to make a fully informed decision, she or he must understand all the risks and benefits of the procedure and the likelihood of success.

17. Beneficence: The practitioner should act in "the best interest" of the patient; the procedure should be provided with the intent of doing good to the patient.

18. Non-maleficence: Above all, do no harm. Make sure that the trial or procedure does not harm the patient or others in society.

Composition of the Ethics Committee:

The composition must be multi-disciplinary, multi-sectorial, and adequate for its functioning.

The IEC should consist of a reasonable number of members who collectively have the qualifications and experience to review and evaluate the scientific, medical, and ethical aspects of the proposed clinical trial.

It is recommended that the Ethics committee include

At least 5 members

1. At least one member whose primary area of interest is in a nonscientific area

2. **Layperson:**
   - A person who does not have specialised or professional knowledge of the subject

   A person who is a non-expert in a given field of knowledge

4. A layperson is one who does not have the qualifications of an expert, e.g., a lawyer, doctor, scientist, or chartered accountant.

5. At least one member who is independent of the Institution.

6. Basic Medical Scientist: The basic sciences include anatomy, physiology, biochemistry, molecular biology, pharmacology, microbiology, and pathology.

As per the Central Drugs Standard Control Organisation's (CDSCO) guidelines for registration of the Ethics Committee (EC), a basic medical scientist should have post-graduate qualifications and adequate experience in his/her respective field.

A basic medical scientist should have an MD in one of the basic sciences.

An MBBS-qualified person cannot serve as a basic medical scientist.

A non-medical person cannot serve as a basic medical scientist.

- CHAIRPERSON
- CLINICIAN
- LEGAL EXPERT/RETIRED JUDGE
- SOCIAL SCIENTIST/REPRESENTATIVE from a non-government voluntary agency
- PHILOSOPHER/ETHICIST/ THEOLOGIAN

TABLE No. 01. Summarizing Principles of Ethics in Clinical Research	
Respect for autonomy	Information about risks/benefits to be provided to study participants
Beneficence Non-maleficence	'best interest of the patient' Do NO harm
Conflict of interest	Policy to be present
Informed consent	Study participants ability to make their own decisions
Confidentiality	Of study participants to be maintained
SAE	Must be addressed

- There should be a documented Term of reference for the appointment, reconstitution, and Resignation of members.
- The Ethics Committee may be reconstituted every 2 years or earlier, as defined in the SOPs.
- The IEC assigns responsibilities to its members with the aim of involving every member in the decision-making process.
- The members shall be trained on the IEC SOPs.
- Conflicts of Interest and Confidentiality shall be addressed at the time of composition.

CAN AN EC MEMBER FULFIL TWO REPRESENTATIONS IN THE QUORUM, SUCH AS SOCIAL WORKER AND LAY PERSON?

No. A person cannot represent two categories listed in the quorum. The representation has to be decided when the EC is formed, and should be documented in the composition and Standard Operating Procedures with clear representation. An EC member cannot change the representation during the EC meeting.

IF A LAY PERSON IS ABSENT FOR PROTOCOL REVIEW MEETINGS, CAN THE MEMBER SECRETARY OF THE IEC OR ANY IEC MEMBER ACT AS A LAY PERSON?

No. This is not acceptable. A person designated as a "Lay person" in EC composition must be present to fulfil the quorum requirements. Nobody else can act as a layperson unless he/she is serving as a layperson in the EC and has been mentioned in the composition. If a layperson is absent, the quorum is not filled, and the EC approval is invalid.

WHAT IS QUORUM?

The quorum is the count of the number of members present in the EC meeting.

A quorum is the minimum number of officers and members of a committee or organization usually a majority, who must be present for a valid transaction of business.

If the number present falls below the required number, the quorum fails.

If any member category defined in Schedule Y Appendix VIII is absent, the requirement of a quorum will not be met.

If an investigator is part of the quorum of five members and is unable to vote for his own study, the quorum will fail.

RECENT CHALLENGE DUE TO TECHNOLOGY ADVANCEMENT:
THE ETHICAL AND LEGAL ISSUES OF ARTIFICIAL INTELLIGENCE

Systems that use AI technologies are becoming autonomous in terms of the complexity of the tasks they can perform, their potential impact on the world, and the diminishing ability of humans to understand, predict, and control their functioning.

There are numerous options in terms of regulation. Technologies that use AI can be regulated as items subject to copyright.

ISSUES AND CONCERNS OF CONDUCTING CLINICAL RESEARCH IN INDIA:

Issues like approval delays, deficiencies in the functioning of CROs and other stakeholders, liabilities and compensation to injured subjects, and insurance issues remain prevalent in India. Hence, multinational companies are rethinking opting for India to conduct clinical trials.

There is a need for the law to ensure that the subjects involved in research are not exploited, are well informed about the risks, and are provided with clarity on regulations.

CONCLUSION:

As clinical research becomes increasingly global-ised, there is a need to make research culturally and methodologically valid. The gap between developed and developing countries needs to be narrowed in order to ensure global justice. The emphasis is to ensure that research ethics are made an integral part of all biomedical research.

There are still many ethical issues in the field of clinical research that need to be addressed.

For instance, there are concerns surrounding stem cell research due to the use of human embryos to harvest stem cells. Moreover, human gene editing research opens the possibility of editing human embryos, another ethical concern that needs to be addressed in the future.

REFERENCES:

1. NIH. (2021). Ethics in clinical research [Online]. Available
   at: https://clinicalcenter.nih.gov/recruit/ethics html

2. Nardini, C., et al. (2014). The ethics of clinical trials. ecancer, 8:387.

3. Shafiq, N., Malhotra, S. (2011). Ethics in clinical research: Need for assessing comprehension of informed consent form? Contemporary Clinical Trials, 32: 169-172.

4. Gowree gokhale, Milind anatani (2016), Issues and concerns in conducting Clinical Trials in India, Pharma Focus Asia

5. Asaro P, " From Mechanisms of Adaptation to Intelligence Amplifiers: The Philosophy of W Ross Ashby" in Wheeler M, Husbands P and Holland O(eds).The Mechanical Mind in History, Cambridge MA, MIT press,149-184, 2014

6. Hage J. Theoritical Foundations for the Responsibility of Autonomous Agents// Artificial Intelligence Law.2017,No 25(3), 255-271.

7. U Pagallo , The Laws of Robots, Crimes, Contracts and Torts, Springer, 2013, 36.

8. Guideline for Good Clinical Practice (resource material)

9. Program on implementation of NABH accreditation standards for ethics committees (course notes)

Chapter 09

Ethics Committee: Responsibilities, Functioning, Approval and Records Management

Mrs. Vaishali Deshpande
Independent Consultant Clinical Research,
Chairperson, Ethics committee, Ruby hall clinic, Sancheti Hospital,
Joshi Hospital, Pune, Maharashtra, Ex research officer at Diabetes unit, KEM Hospital research centre,
Mumbai., Maharashtra.

Abstract

In the era of clinical research and human trials, safety and data protection of the participants along with the adherence of the studies to the ethical guidelines and regulations has become questionable. Thus, establishment of the ethics committee has become mandatory to regulate the clinical research trials and maintain the transparency and confidentiality of the clinical research and the data.

Ethics committee plays important role in addressing ethical issues that arise in patient care and facilitate sound decision making that respects participants' values, concerns, and interests. It helps in Reviewing research proposals involving human participants and their data, to ensure that they are in accordance with local and international ethical guidelines and regulations. Ethics committee assist in ethics related educational programming and policy development within the institutions. It helps in Monitoring studies and ongoing clinical research trials, and follow-up actions after the end of the research, in case of need.

Introduction

The word "ethics" is derived from the Greek word ethos (character), and from the Latin word morals (customs). Ethics (1,2) is a branch of philosophy that deals with questions of right and wrong. It explores the nature of morality and provide rational and systematic approach to decision-making. By adhering to ethical standards, researchers can strike a balance between scientific progress and the protection of human rights, ensuring that research benefits society while maintaining the dignity and well-being of participants.

When we follow ethics, it helps us to inculcate societal thinking and human behaviour in research. For an instance, for infectious diseases like tuberculosis or HIV, whether to prioritize privacy of patients or consider benefits of society at large is a very sensitive issue. Overall, the study of ethics fosters critical thinking, empathy, and moral reasoning. This helps individuals to navigate ethical challenges and contribute to the well -being of themselves and others in a morally responsible manner. Ethical guidelines for clinical research include social and clinical value, scientific validity, fair subject selection, favourable risk-benefit ratio, independent review, informed consent, and respect for potential and enrolled participants.

Although we all are familiar with the Ethical or moral principals, the atrocities that taken place in the past lead to the establishment of the guidelines and regulations. Following are a few examples which are responsible for the current stringent regulations. **Nuremberg Code (1947)(8):** The Nuremberg Code emerged in response to the atrocities committed during World War II, particularly the unethical experiments conducted by Nazi physicians. The code established ten principles that form the foundation of modern ethical standards in clinical research. These principles include the requirement for voluntary informed consent, the necessity of research to be based on sound scientific principles, and the avoidance of unnecessary harm to participants. This gave birth to CONCEPT OF CONSENT. **Thalidomide Tragedy** (1950s-1960s)(9): The thalidomide tragedy, where a medication caused severe birth defects, had a profound impact on the regulation of clinical trials .

Corresponding author: Mrs. Vaishali Deshpande. Can be contacted at phone number+91 93260 22386

Email id: vaishalideshpande21@gmail.com

It highlighted the need for rigorous preclinical testing, comprehensive safety assessments, and stringent monitoring of potential risks. The tragedy led to the establishment of more stringent regulations and safety standards in clinical trials, especially in the field of drug development. Tuskegee Syphilis Study (1932-1972): **The Tuskegee Syphilis Study**, conducted in the United States, was a notorious example of unethical research. African American men with syphilis were left untreated and were not informed about the nature of the study. The study's revelation led to significant reforms in research ethics. Declaration of Helsinki (1964): **The Declaration of Helsinki(7)** was established by the World Medical Association and is one of the most influential and first international ethical guidelines for biomedical research. It has undergone multiple revisions and updates since its inception. The declaration outlines ethical principles for physicians and researchers and again emphasizing the importance of informed consent, protection of vulnerable populations, and the necessity of research ethics committees. **Belmont Report** (1979) (10): The Belmont Report was a response to the Tuskegee study and provided a comprehensive ethical framework for research involving human subjects. It identified three fundamental principles i.e. respect for persons, beneficence, and justice and a recently added no harm principal. The report emphasized the importance of informed consent, minimizing risks, and ensuring fairness in the selection of research participants.

As mentioned above, clinical and health research is a major component of human ethics. The following are key historical developments in the evolution of ethics in clinical trials:

International Council on Harmonization (ICH) Guidelines(3): The ICH is an international organization that develops guidelines for the pharmaceutical industry. The ICH guidelines, particularly Good Clinical Practice (GCP) guidelines, provide an unified ethical and scientific standard for the design, conduct, monitoring, and reporting of the clinical trials. These guidelines address various aspects, including informed consent, participant safety, data integrity, and the responsibilities of researchers and sponsors. In India, Indian Council Of Medical Research (ICMR) has given National Ethical Guidelines(2017) (8) for Biomedical and Health research. Recently ICMR has released Ethical Guidelines for Application of Artificial Intelligence in Biomedical Research and Healthcare in 2023.

Regulatory Bodies and Guidelines: Regulatory bodies, such as the U.S. Food and Drug Administration (FDA), European Medicines Agency (EMA), Central Drugs Standard Control Organization (CDSCO) (6)

and other national and international agencies, have established regulations and guidelines to ensure the ethical conduct of clinical trials. These regulations provide oversight, define ethical standards, and require the submission of comprehensive protocols and documentation before initiating clinical research to regulatory authorities and Institutional Review Board / Institutional Ethics Committee.

Ethics in research refers to the principles, guidelines, and standards that govern the conduct of scientific investigations involving human participants. It involves a set of moral considerations and responsibilities to ensure that research is conducted in an ethical and responsible manner. Thus, the ethics committee was established to ensure that these regulations and ethical guidelines are followed.

Ethics Committee: importance, responsibilities, Functioning, Approval Process and Records Management.

An ethics committee is a group of individuals from diverse backgrounds who support health care institutions or other organizations with various functions related to ethical issues. Ethics committees are often involved in clinical trials, research projects, patient care, organizational policies and conflict resolution. The main role of an ethics committee is to protect the rights, safety and well-being of human subjects involved in any activity that has ethical implications.

In 2019, the Indian regulatory authorities established a separate ethics committee for the academic clinical trial/ research. The Ethics Committee, which is registered under DCGI, will only look after the Clinical Trials and BABE studies, and the ethics Committee which is registered under the Department of Health Research (DHR) will look after the academic trials/research. As per the regulatory requirement of India which has been given by the new clinical trial rules (2019), to establish an ethics committee, there has to be at least seven members in the committee.

The details of the members of the ethics committee and their qualification is as follows- (8)

Table No 01. Type of ethics committee members and their qualifications.

Members of EC	Qualifications
Chairperson/ Vice Chairperson (optional) Non-affiliated	A well-respected person from any background with prior experience of having served/serving in an EC.
Member Secretary/ Alternate Member Secretary (optional) Affiliated	Should be a staff member of the institution. Should have knowledge and experience in clinical research and ethics, be motivated and have good communication skills. Should be able to devote adequate time to this activity which should be protected by the institution
Basic Medical Scientist(s) Affiliated/ non-affiliated	Non-medical or medical person with qualifications in basic medical sciences. In case of EC reviewing clinical trials with drugs, the basic medical scientist should preferably be a pharmacologist.
Clinician(s) Affiliated/ non-affiliated	Should be individual/s with recognized medical qualification, expertise and training.
Legal expert/s Affiliated/ non-affiliated	Should have a basic degree in Law from a recognized university, with experience. Desirable: Training in medical law.
Social scientist/ philosopher/ ethicist/theologian Affiliated/ non-affiliated	Should be an individual with social/behavioural science/philosophy/ religious qualification and training and/or expertise and be sensitive to local cultural and moral values. Can be from an NGO involved in health-related activities
Lay person(s) Non-affiliated	Literate person who has not pursued a medical science/ health related career in the last 5 years. May be a representative of the community and aware of the local language, cultural and moral values of the community Desirable: involved in social and community welfare activities

Responsibilities of an Ethics Committee

Some of the common responsibilities of an ethics committee are:

- To review and approve the protocol, informed consent form, recruitment materials and other documents related to a clinical trial or research project before it starts, and monitor its progress and compliance with ethical standards.

To provide guidance and consultation to researchers, health care professionals, patients, families and other stakeholders on ethical dilemmas or questions arising from the activity.

- To set and oversee the rules for the conduct of the organization and its members, and provide accountability for their behavior.
- To promote fair and ethical policies and procedures within the organization and among its partners and collaborators.
- To enhance the ethical culture and awareness among the organization and its members, and foster ethical education and training.

- To resolve conflicts or complaints related to ethical issues, and impose sanctions or disciplinary actions when necessary.

Functioning of an Ethics Committee

The functioning of an ethics committee may vary depending on its type, scope, mandate and context. However, some general principles that guide the functioning of an ethics committee are:

- The ethics committee should have a clear term of reference that define its purpose, objectives, functions, composition, procedures and authority.
- The ethics committee should have a diverse and multidisciplinary membership that reflects the relevant expertise, perspectives and interests of the stakeholders involved in or affected by the activity under review.
- The ethics committee should have an independent and impartial status that allows it to exercise its judgment without undue influence or pressure from any party.
- The ethics committee should follow a transparent and consistent process that ensures fair and timely review and decision-making based on ethical principles and standards.
- The ethics committee should maintain confidentiality and respect for the privacy of the participants, researchers, health care professionals and other parties involved in or affected by the activity under review.
- The ethics committee should document its activities, decisions, rationales and recommendations, and communicate them effectively to the relevant parties.

The ethics committee should evaluate its performance regularly and seek feedback from its stakeholders to improve its quality and effectiveness.

Approval Process of an Ethics Committee

The approval process of an ethics committee may vary depending on the type, scope, complexity and risk level of the activity under review. However, some general steps that are involved in the approval process are:

- The researcher or health care professional submits an application to the ethics committee that includes the protocol, informed consent form, recruitment materials and other relevant documents related to the activity under review.
- The ethics committee screens the application for completeness, eligibility and compliance with ethical standards.
- The ethics committee assigns reviewers to assess the application based on their expertise, experience and availability.

- The reviewers conduct a thorough review of the application using a checklist or a set of criteria that covers various aspects such as scientific validity, risk-benefit analysis, informed consent process, participant protection measures, data management plan etc.
- The reviewers submit their comments, questions or recommendations to the ethics committee for further discussion or clarification.
- The ethics committee convenes a meeting to deliberate on the application based on the reviewers' inputs and other relevant information. The meeting may be held in person or online depending on the feasibility and preference of the members. The meeting may also involve inviting external experts or stakeholders for consultation or input if needed.
- The ethics committee reaches a consensus or a majority vote on whether to approve, reject or request modifications to the application. The decision may be conditional or unconditional depending on the nature and extent of the issues identified by the reviewers or during the meeting.
- The ethics committee communicates its decision along with its rationale and recommendations to the researcher or health care professional in writing within a specified time frame. The decision may also be communicated to other parties such as sponsors, regulators or funders if required by law or agreement.
- The researcher or health care professional acknowledges receipt of the decision and complies with any conditions or modifications requested by the ethics committee before starting or continuing the activity under review. The researcher or health care professional also reports any changes, deviations or adverse events that occur during the course of the activity to the ethics committee for further review or action.
- Additionally, the ethics committee grants approval of a proposal in the format of Approval, Conditional approval and rejection.

Records Management of an Ethics Committee

The records management of an ethics committee refers to the creation, maintenance, storage, retrieval, preservation and disposal of the records related to the activities and decisions of the ethics committee. The records management of an ethics committee is important for ensuring accountability, transparency, quality and compliance with ethical standards. As per New Drug clinical Trial rule (NDCTR,2019) ethics committee should retain the documents for five years. Some of the best practices for records management of an ethics committee are:

- The ethics committee should have a records management policy that defines the types, formats,

- contents, ownership, access, retention and disposal of the records related to the activities and decisions of the ethics committee.
- The ethics committee should designate a person or a team to be responsible for the records management of the ethics committee. The person or team should have the necessary skills, knowledge and resources to perform the records management tasks effectively and efficiently.
- The ethics committee should create and maintain accurate, complete and up-to-date records of its activities and decisions using appropriate tools and systems. The records should include but not limited to the application forms, protocols, informed consent forms, recruitment materials, review reports, meeting minutes, decision letters, correspondence, feedback forms etc.
- The ethics committee should store and secure the records in a safe and accessible location that protects them from unauthorized access, alteration, damage or loss. The ethics committee should also backup the records regularly and have a contingency plan in case of emergencies or disasters.
- The ethics committee should retrieve and provide the records to the authorized parties upon request or as required by law or agreement. The ethics committee should also ensure that the records are used only for legitimate purposes and that the confidentiality and privacy of the parties involved are respected.

Conclusion

Overall, ethics committee play a pivotal role in maintaining protection, confidentiality, well-being and safety of the research participants. It ensures no harm to the mankind and provides seamless and well-regulated functioning of a clinical research and human participation.

References
1. https://www.britannica.com/topic/ethics
2. https://www.bbc.co.uk/ethics/introduction/intro
3. https://database.ich.org/sites/default/files/E6_R2_Addendum.pdf
4. https://www.indiascienceandtechnology.gov.in/sites/default/files/file-uploads/guidelineregulations/1527507675_ICMR_Ethical_Guidelines_2017.pdf
5. https://main.icmr.nic.in/sites/default/files/upload_documents/Ethical_Guidelines_AI_Healthcare_2023.pdf
6. https://cdsco.gov.in/opencms/opencms/en/Clinical-Trial/Ethics-Committee/
7. https://www.wma.net/policies-post/wma-declaration-of-helsinki-ethical-principles-for-medical-research-involving-human-subjects/
8. Book Nazi medicine and the ethics of human research www.thelancet.com Vol 366 September 3, 2005 Julia Neuberger
9. https://en.wikipedia.org/wiki/Thalidomide
10. https://www.hhs.gov/ohrp/regulations-and-policy/belmont-report/index.html

Chapter 10

A Patient's Perspective – Clinical Trial Challenges and Concerns

Mrs. Renuka Neogi B. Pharm, MSc (CR, ICRI)
Deputy General Manager & Head – Global Clinical Quality Management,
Global Clinical Development, Sun Pharma Industries Limited
Bhairavi A-103, Doordarshan CHS, Gokuldham, Goregaon East,

Abstract

The Patient is one of the most important stakeholders in any clinical trial. It is important, that patients are well informed, protected and treated well, as this will have a direct impact on patient's recruitment and retention in the trial.

While the clinical research industry is adopting several technological advances, it is becoming increasingly critical to understand the concerns and challenges being faced by the patients. This will help the clinical research industry (Sponsors, CROs, Investigators, Sites, SMOs, Ethics Committees, Regulators) to come up with solutions, which will not only allay patients' concerns but also lead to successful delivery of clinical trials.

CHALLENGES and CONCERNS

Every Sponsor, CRO and Investigator have 2 pertinent questions in their mind at the start of the trial **WHY** would a patient participate in a trial and **HOW** do we get patients participating in the trial?

Answer to "WHY" is relatively simple, as there are anticipated benefits. However, answer to "HOW" is difficult. Informed Consent Document (ICD) helps in answering "HOW", as it respects autonomy. This elaborative document when handed over to the patient / legally acceptable representative (LAR) for their reading, seems very long, complex & uninteresting. India is a diverse country and is growing socially, economically and globally. The latest census done in India was in 2011, revealed the country literacy rate of 74.04%. *(For the purpose of census 2011, a person aged 7 and above, who can both read and write with understanding in any language, is treated as literate.)* While the literate and illiterate population. This level is further impacted given the circumstances in which the independence, there is a significant percentage of population which is still illiterate. Also, the level of comprehension is always a question with both literate and illiterate population. This level is further impacted given the circumstances in which the patient /LAR is offered a chance to participate in the trial.

Patients / LAR may have several concerns in their minds, due to which decision making could become difficult. Patients could be unsure of the treatment option they could receive (in case of randomized and blinded studies), anxious about the safety and efficacy of the trial treatment, worried about the worsening of disease, if allocated a placebo arm. They could be stressed, due to numerous hospital visits, long waiting hours, several blood draws and complex trial specific procedures, including study drug management in temperature-controlled conditions at home. There are possibilities of daily

Corresponding author: Mrs. Renuka Neogi. Can be contacted at phone number+91 99679 68614.
Email id: renuka182001@gmail.com

routine being impacted due to trial participation e.g. students missing out on their school and extra-curricular activities and working patients unable to attend offices, take leaves and decreased work productivity. There could be a feeling of embarrassment when doctor speaks about contraception (per protocol requirement) with the unmarried potential patients. Shyness seeps in, when it comes to facing the camera for AV recording of informed consent. There could be a fear of spoiling the doctor-patient relationships (if declined to participate in the trial / premature withdrawal during the course of the trial). If patients have to perform certain tasks digitally e.g. completion of electronic diaries, use of wearables etc. there could be some discomforts, as technological adoption is not easy for all. Uncertainty about the future and 'what will happen to my family, if something happens to me?" haunts patients' minds. To add to these woes, social - religious – cultural – economical barriers, media publicity and general perceptions about clinical trials, confidentiality issues make patients / LAR confused and apprehensive.

Other common questions like management of screen-failure patients (emotional and treatments), post-trial accesses etc. continue to remain debatable. While companies and investigators are now coming up with newer strategies and tools for recruitment, a patient centric approach needs to be established for their successful retention in the trials and compliance to the trial procedures.

SOLUTIONS

It is important to develop solutions around these challenges & concerns by identifying the influencers (main reasons to participate) and motivators (what would make the patients happy) for the patients.

Soft Skills, Emotional Quotient, Attitudes and Behaviors are now essentials for building a good doctor-patient relationship. Patients / LARs should be dealt with care, patience, empathy, respect, calmness and pathways should be created for open, honest and transparent dialogues.

If the patients are made to walk through the clinical trial journey at the beginning and later on, and at regular intervals; it will help the patients to understand, visualize and be better prepared for their trial experience. Trial protocols, if prepared with a patient centric approach or, if the companies collaborate with patient support groups and solicit feedbacks on their protocol, will help in the identification and resolution of issues early on. Implement components of decentralized clinical trials (as appropriate) e.g., Reduce on-site patient visits by introducing telemedicine or frequent virtual calls with the trial doctor and site staff; or introducing home nursing option, where biological lab sampling and study drug administration can happen from patients' residence or collaborating with diagnostic labs at multiple locations, thus allowing patients to perform complex diagnostics e.g., MRI etc. from nearby location. Implement simple & yet effective technological solutions e.g., wearables for measurement and transmission of vitals and other parameters, or electronic patient diaries.

Small initiatives like greeting patients on their birthdays / anniversaries, appreciating them for their participation, reminders on smart phones before visit, priority access to doctor, pre-arranged transportation and meals for their hospital visit, providing lab report copies, issue reimbursement in an expedited manner, taking extra care of vulnerable patients, updating patients about their progress, conducting home visits, making them ambassadors of clinical trials (post trial completion) and provide them opportunities of counselling or experience sharing with other patients, inviting them as lay persons in Ethics Committee or to support patient advocacy groups (where possible and if found capable) etc. will help the overall clinical research industry in enhancing patient experiences'.

Regular health status update by the trial doctor to the patient's family physician will help in assuring the patient, that an appropriate ecosystem is put in place with his /her treatment and safety at the cornerstone.

PATIENTS' RESPONSIBILITIES and RIGHTS

While the clinical research industry along with the support of regulators, public and private organizations, advocacy groups are putting in measures to safeguard patients; it is also important for the patients to understand their own rights and responsibilities.

Patients should provide to the best of his/her knowledge, complete information and current medical condition and past medical history. Patients should read & understand the ICD in detail and discuss the trial with investigators and site staff. They should ask questions and ensure that their doubts are well answered. Rather than signing the ICD in the first meeting itself, patients should take some time out and discuss the trial with their family and family doctor. ICD should be signed only, if the patient voluntarily agrees to participate after having understood all the relevant aspects of the trial.

Once enrolled, it is important that the patients follow the doctors'/site staff instructions and cooperate with them, take their medicines properly, follow the trial schedule and procedures. If the patients are unable to come for a visit or would miss or has missed the medication dose; should promptly inform the doctor. They should not take any other medications without consulting their trial doctor. Patients should carry all trial supplies (used & unused medicines, diaries, devices etc.) during their hospital visits for verification. They should promptly report to the doctor any unexpected problems / changes in their medical condition. Utmost precautions to be taken for storage of trial medications in a secured place at home and per the temperature requirement specified in the ICD. Unused medications / supplies should not be distributed to other family members / friends; but be returned to the doctor at the end of the trial. Patients should submit any bills (lab tests, travel etc.) in a timely manner.

Patients should be aware of their following rights –
- Right to Accessibility, availability and continuity of care and safety
- Right to Dignity, Confidentiality and Privacy
- Right to Information and education
- Right to express any preferences e.g. social, cultural, spiritual
- Right to refusal of treatment
- Right to get protection
- Right to give informed consent and withdrawal from the trial
- Right to Complain and Redressal
- Right to access his/her own medical records
- Right to take a second opinion and discuss with family/relatives and family doctor
- Right to know hospital rules and regulations

Simple training videos on disease, trial procedures, roles & responsibilities of patients will be very helpful to improve patients' understanding of their clinical trial journey.

Conclusion:

To conclude on this topic, it is important that the industry is cognizant of the patients' perspectives and feelings towards clinical trials. Continuous efforts must be made to disseminate appropriate information in a simplified manner, make the patients aware of their rights and responsibilities and set the expectations right in the beginning of the patient-doctor collaboration. Oversight from the Ethics Committees and seeking regular feedback on patients' experiences by investigators / patient support groups / hospital attached social workers, will not only help in safeguarding patients' rights, safety and wellbeing; but also, in their participation and retention in the clinical trials.

References:
1. Bhatt, Arun. India's next challenge: Rebooting recruitment. Perspectives in Clinical Research 5 (3):p 93-94, Jul–Sep 2014. | DOI: 10.4103/2229-3485.134295
2. https://knowindia.india.gov.in/profile/literacy.php
3. https://www.census2011.co.in/literacy.php
4. Chaudhari, Nayan; Ravi, Renju; Gogtay, Nithya J.; Thatte, Urmila M.. Recruitment and retention of the participants in clinical trials: Challenges and solutions. Perspectives in Clinical Research 11(2):p 64-69, Apr–Jun 2020. | DOI: 10.4103/picr.PICR_206_19

6. https://www.kokilabenhospital.com/medical_research/research_patient__rights_responsibilities.html

7. https://www.clinicalleader.com/doc/practical-ways-to-improve-the-patient-experience-in-clinical-trials-0001

8. Aljeezan MK, Altaher YY, Boushal TA, Al-sultan AM, Khan AS. Patients' Awareness of Their Rights and Responsibilities: A Cross-Sectional Study From Al-Ahsa. Cureus. 2022 Dec 23;14(12):e32854. doi: 10.7759/cureus.32854. PMID: 36578857; PMCID: PMC9780781.

Acknowledgement: I would like to thank Dr. Shiva Murthy N for providing this opportunity to write this article and Dr. Arun Bhatt for his guidance and continuous motivation.

Disclaimer: The thoughts presented in this chapter are personal opinions of the author. It does not reflect the opinions or views of Sun Pharma or its members.

Source of Support: Nil

Conflict of Interest: None

Chapter 11

Responsibilities of Investigators

Dr. Anuradha H V, MBBS, MD, PGDMLE
Professor & HOD, Department of Pharmacology
Member secretary, Ethics Committee

Abstract

Investigator is the most important person in the conduct of clinical trial and should meet all the expectations of research including qualification, experience and regulatory requirements. Investigator is a person who is responsible for not only conduct of the study, but also the rights, health and welfare of the participants. The investigator can conduct sponsor driven clinical trials and investigator initiated clinical research.

The investigator should be qualified by education as specified by the applicable regulatory requirement training. He / she should have adequate experience to assume responsibility for the proper conduct of the trial and also should be aware of various guidelines

The investigators should be familiar with the investigational product, protocol, investigator's brochure and informed consent keeping in mind to protect the participants rights. In addition, they should also have an awareness of financial aspects, audits, inspections and reporting of serious adverse events within timelines to the necessary stakeholders, etc.

Investigator play a key role in the conduct of clinical trial and has numerous responsibilities and also responsible for the liaison between the sponsor, institution, and the ethics committee.

Keywords: Investigator, Sponsor, ethics committee, informed consent

Introduction: Investigator is the most important person in the conduct of clinical trial and should meet all the expectations of research including qualification, experience and regulatory requirements.[1] An investigator is a person who is responsible for the conduct of the study and for the rights, health and welfare of the participants.

If the study is conducted by a team of investigators, then one person is designated as the Principal Investigator and others as co-investigator and sub-investigator. The investigator can conduct two types of clinical trials; sponsor driven clinical trials and investigator initiated clinical research.

Objective: To understand the roles and responsibilities of investigator for the conduct of clinical trial.

Corresponding author: Dr Anuradha H V. Can be contacted at phone number+91 94488 47946
Email id: dranuradhapharmac@gmail.com

Criteria to be an investigator: [1,2,3]

The investigators should be qualified by education as specified by the applicable regulatory requirement training. They should have adequate experience to assume responsibility for the proper conduct of the trial and also should be aware of International Council for Harmonisation for Good Clinical Practice, Indian Good Clinical Practice, New Drugs and Clinical Trials rules 2019, and Indian Council for Medical Research guidelines. The primary investigator should be qualified medical profession as per by National Medical Council requirement for conducting the clinical trial.

Responsibilities of the investigator(s): [2,3]

1. The investigator should be qualified by education, training, and experience to take up the responsibility for the conduct of the trial and should meet all the qualifications specified by the regulatory requirement.
2. The investigator should be thoroughly familiar with the protocol, investigator brochure, informed consent form and other documents related to the study.
3. The investigator should be aware of International Council for Harmonisation for Good Clinical Practice, Indian Good Clinical Practice, New Drugs and Clinical Trials rules 2019, Medical Device Rules 2017 and Indian Council for Medical Research guidelines.
4. It is the responsibility of the investigator to have qualified persons in his team and train them to delegate the trial / study related work in his absence.
5. The investigator is responsible for supervising any individual or party to whom the investigator delegates trial-related duties and functions for the conduct of the study at the trial site.
6. The investigator should have an adequate time for the conduct of the study.

7. Before initiating a trial, the investigator should have approval from the institutional ethics committee for the trial protocol, investigator brochure, written informed consent form, subject recruitment documents like advertisements), clinical trial agreements and insurance, etc.
8. The investigator should conduct the trial in compliance with the protocol agreed to by the sponsor and approved by the Institutional Ethics Committee.
9. The investigator should not implement any deviation from, or changes of the protocol without agreement by the sponsor and prior approval by the Institutional Ethics Committee of an amendment.
10. The investigator should follow the trial randomisation and blinding procedure as per the protocol.
11. In case of any deviation from the protocol, same should be notified to the Ethics committee with an explanation for the deviation.
12. The investigator should permit to monitor or audit his study by the sponsor.
13. The investigator should also cooperate inspection by the regulatory authorities.
14. The investigator as well as the institution should ensure of providing adequate medical support to the participant in case of occurrence of any adverse event during the course of the study.
15. All adverse events need to be informed to the ethics committee and other stakeholders as per the guidelines within proper timeline.
16. If the participant is not obliged to give reason for withdrawing prematurely from a trial, the investigator should make a reasonable effort to ascertain the reason, fully respecting the subject's rights.

Responsibilities of investigator towards Investigational Product(s): [2,3]

1. It is the responsibility of the primary investigator for the accountability of the investigational product at the trial site.

2. If needed, Principal investigator can assign the duty to another co-investigator and the process need to documented.

3. Proper records of the investigator product regarding delivery to the trial site, inventory at the site, usage by participants and return to the sponsor to be maintained.

4. The investigational product should be stored appropriately as specified by the sponsor and in accordance with the regulatory requirements.

5. The investigational product should be used only by the participants as per the approved protocol

6. The investigator or coinvestigators should guide the participant regarding use of the investigational product as per instructions in the protocol and should be monitored at regular intervals.

Role of investigator during informed consent process of the participants: [2,3]

The investigator should comply with the regulatory requirements, Good Clinical Practice and to the ethical principles as mentioned in the Declaration of Helsinki while obtaining and documenting the informed consent process. If the participant in the trial is a child, assent and consent by the parent or guardian or legally acceptable representative to be obtained as per the regulatory guidelines. The language used in the oral and written information about the trial should be simple and understandable to the participant or the legally acceptable representative and the impartial witness, wherever applicable.

If the informed consent form is amended after addition or deletion of any information in it, the approval has to sought from the institutional ethics committee. Reconsenting to be taken from the participants in case of any amendments. Coercing or unduly influencing the participant to participate or to continue to participate in a trial by the investigators is not acceptable. **Copy of the signed and dated informed consent form should be handed over to the** participant or the legally acceptable representative.

Responsibilities of investigators for records and reports: [2,3]

(a) Records:

The investigator should maintain adequate and accurate source documents and trial records that include all pertinent observations about trial participants. Source data should be attributable, legible, original, accurate, and complete. The investigator should ensure the completeness, legibility, and timeliness of the data reported to the sponsor in the case record forms and other required reports. The investigator/institution should take measures to prevent accidental or premature destruction of these documents and all documents to be archived in a safe place for a minimum period of 5 years after the completion of the trial. Upon request of the monitor, auditor, ethics committee, or regulatory authority, the investigator should make available for direct access all requested trial-related records.

(b) Progress Reports:

The investigator should submit written summaries of the trial status to the ethics committee periodically, half yearly and annually as per the standard operating procedures of the ethics committee. In case of any changes significantly affecting the trial or causing increase risk to the participants, the same has to be communicated to the sponsor and the ethics committee without fail. Upon completion of the trial, the investigator should inform the institution & should provide the ethics committee with a summary of the trial's outcome, and the detailed report to the regulatory authority.

(c) Safety Reports:

All adverse effects should be reported to the ethics committee on periodic basis. Serious adverse events (SAEs) should be reported immediately or within 24 hours as the New Drugs and Cinical Trials rules,2019 to the sponsor, ethics committee and the regulators. The immediate reports should be followed promptly by detailed, written reports within 14 days of initial reporting.

Role of investigator in premature termination / suspension of a trial: [2,3]

If the trial is prematurely terminated or suspended for any reason, the investigator should promptly inform the trial subjects, should assure appropriate therapy and follow-up for the participants. If the investigator terminates or suspends a trial without prior agreement of the sponsor, the investigator should inform the institution; and the investigator/institution should promptly inform the sponsor and the Ethics Committee, and should provide the sponsor and the ethics committee a detailed written explanation of the termination or suspension. If the sponsor terminates or suspends a trial, the investigator should promptly inform the institution and the ethics committee. If the ethics committee terminates or suspends its approval of a trial, the investigator should inform the institution and the investigator/institution should promptly notify the sponsor and provide the sponsor with a detailed written explanation of the termination or suspension.

Conclusion: Investigator play a key role in the conduct of clinical trial and has numerous responsibilities as he is primarily involved in taking approval of trial documents from the institutional ethics committee, in contact with the participants of the trial, maintain of trial related documents; and also responsible for the liaison between the sponsor, institution, ethics committee and the regulatory authority.

References:
1. Baer AR, Devine S, Beardmore CD and Catalano R. Clinical investigator responsibilities. Journal of Oncology Practice 2011; 1(2): 124-128.
2. https://database.ich.org/sites/default/files/ICH_E6%28R3%29_DraftGuideline_2023_0519.pdf
3. https://cdsco.gov.in/opencms/export/sites/CDSCO_WEB/Pdf-documents/NewDrugs_CTRules_2019.pdf

Chapter 12

Roles and Responsibilities of Site Management Organization (SMO) in Clinical Trials

Mr. Snehendu Koner, MA (American Lit, Stanley Ind, USA),
Head, Business Development, CliniMed LifeSciences,
Regional Coordinator, India, Avoidable Deaths Network (ADN),
Kolkata, West Bengal.

Abstract

A site management organization delivers operational and administrative support services on behalf of the clinical investigator at a clinical research site to contract research organization (CRO) , pharmaceutical company, biotechnology company, and medical device company by handling start-up, regulatory compliance activities, patient recruitment & follow-up, study documentation preparation, reporting of adverse events or serious adverse events if any (AE / SAE), data collection till closeout, and study document archival activities with their adequate infrastructure and staff to meet the requirements of the clinical trial protocol. Site Management Organizations are expected to adapt optimal Decentralized Clinical Trial (DCT) / Virtual Clinical Trial (VCT) solutions to reduce the burden on patients and conduct clinical trial efficiently. The global clinical trial SMO market size was valued at USD 5572 million in 2021 and is expected to expand at a CAGR of 6.1% from 2022 to 2030. This market is growing because of rising R&D investments by pharmaceutical companies due to high burden of chronic and infectious diseases. Apart from this, the Covid pandemic has contributed lot to the need for clinical trials, which is one of the key factors in the recent SMO market growth. With this background, SMOs role in CT management is discussed in this article.

Objective

A site management organization delivers operational and administrative support services on behalf of the clinical investigator at a clinical research site to contract research organization (CRO) , pharmaceutical company , biotechnology company and medical device company by handling start-up, regulatory compliance activities, patient recruitment & follow-up, study documentation preparation, reporting of adverse events or serious adverse events if any (AE / SAE) and data collection till closeout and study documents archival activities with their adequate infrastructure and staff to meet the requirements of the clinical trial protocol.

Benefits of working with SMO:
1. SMO attracts sponsors of CROs for the new studies to the sites and SMO team participate actively in site identification and selection process in collaboration with the principal investi-

2. Centralized administration is managed by SMO.
3. SMO does contract negotiation on behalf of the sites.
4. Responsible for entire subject recruitment activities which is one of the important keys to success of any clinical trials.
5. SMO maintains centralized database of potential subjects for upcoming studies.
6. Manage and follow up sponsor payments.
7. Support in project specific training
8. Staffing, hire, train and compensate site employees (clinical research coordinators, sub-investigators, study nurses, etc)
9. QA and QC activities at site level

The importance of Site management Organization (SMO) comes into picture in order to attract more pharmaceutical companies to outsource their clinical trials in India.

Corresponding author: Mr. Snehendu Koner. Can be contacted at phone number+91 89107 27706
Email id: snehendu.koner@clinimedlifesciences.com

SMOs are relatively new conferee aiming at providing economical conduct of clinical trials maintaining all regulatory compliances with utmost quality within the stringent timeline. SMOs usually have a network of clinical research sites which they manage at their own based on their understanding and agreement with the head of the clinical research site which may be a government or private hospitals/sites.

Sometime we can see some fly-by-night site management organisations are being run by 1-2 coordinators or staffs which should not be the case. SMOs must have at least one registered office in the particular state/city where they are running the sites (private or government hospitals) and at least a minimum number of experienced employees with structured organogram. They should have their own SOPs in place apart from the site SOP. There are many investigators conducting clinical trials for the first time. SMOs are playing a great role here. They are assisting investigators with day-to-day study activities following the protocol, ICH-GCP standards and helping to provide high-quality data to the sponsors / CROs. The majority of the data accepted by supreme regularity authorities like US-FDA is coming from the sites/studies where SMO is involved. The SMO is not only a necessity for busy clinicians or investigators but also ensures quality data management.

So, I think, the sponsors or CROs should check SMO's capabilities and experience upfront before selection of SMO for any site for any study. Sponsors should check how organized the organization, how many studies already conducted by them and how many subjects recruited in their completed or ongoing study and whether any audits by any sponsor or regulatory authorities conducted for their studies earlier and what was the outcome for the same.

There is also a serious concern related to hybrid organizations that offer both CRO and SMO services especially the site monitoring activities.

A single company cannot objectively monitor the performance of its own sites and coordinators as it is responsible for the outcome of the study. So, the distinct SMO model is necessary in India. In fact, the subject enrolment issues cited by almost every global company relating to the clinical research have virtually disappeared now-a-days after the SMO came into picture.

Now onwards all the CROs has to be registered and will go through DCGI inspections, though it is not finalized yet while I am writing this abstract (July 20, 2023) , as of now it is in the draft status and under discussion or considerations. We all agree that Indeed it is a welcome initiative, if it doesn't become red tapism. Now question is will SMO also be requiring registration? In fact, the SMO is a service provider that offers the clinical investigators at a study site operations and administrative support. Hence if SMO is limited to these services, then there might not be requirement of the registration. In short, SMOs are contracted generally by CROs and treated as vendor therefore their registration is not a mandatory.

Site Management Organization should adapt optimal Decentralized Clinical Trial (DCT) / Virtual Clinical Trial (VCT) solutions to reduce the burden on patients and conduct clinical trial efficiently. The global clinical trial SMO market size was valued at USD 5572 million in 2021 and is expected to expand at a CAGR of 6.1% from 2022 to 2030 . This market is grown just because of rising R&D investments by pharmaceutical companies due to high burden of chronic and infectious diseases. Apart from this, the Covid pandemic has contributed lot to the need for clinical trials which is one of the key factor of this recent time SMO market growth.

Table No. 01 - Clinical Trials Site Management Organizations Market Report Scope

Report Attribute	Details
Market Size value in 2022	USD 5.9 billion
Revenue forecast in 2030	USD 9.5 billion
Growth rate	CAGR 6.1 % from 2022 to 2030
Base year for estimation	2021
Historical data	2018 - 2020
Forecast period	2022 - 2030
Quantitative units	Revenue in USD million and CAGR from 2021 to 2030
Report coverage	Revenue forecast, company ranking, competitive landscape, growth factors, and trends
Segments covered	Clinical trial services/components, phase, therapeutic areas, region
Regional scope	North America; Europe; Asia Pacific; Latin America; Middle East & Africa
Country scope	U.S.; Canada; U.K.; Germany; France; Italy; Spain; India; Japan; China; Australia; South Korea; Brazil; Mexico; Argentina; Colombia; South Africa; Saudi Arabia; UAE
Report coverage	Revenue forecast, company share, competitive landscape, growth factors, and trends
Key companies profiled	Clinedge; WCG; ClinChoice; Access Clinical Research; FOMAT Medical Research INC.; SGS; KV Clinical; SMO-Pharmina; Xylem Clinical Research; Aurum Clinical Research
Customization scope	Free report customization (equivalent up to 8 analysts' working days) with purchase. Addition or alteration to country, regional, and segment scope.

The Asia specific region especially India has become a hotspot for conducting clinical trials due to the ease of regulatory compliance, cheap costs, a growing patient population, and the existence of a few elite clinical institutions functioning as sites. These factors are supporting the demand for site management services which promotes the market for SMO. Mergers, acquisitions, and partnerships in between SMO and CRO or sponsors should be the key strategies to be adopted by the site management organizations to develop the services like site identification, site feasibility, and clinical monitoring.

Reference :

For SMO market size data ~ source: www.grandviewresearch.com

Chapter 13

Contents Of Informed Consent Document and Consenting Procedures (Methodology)

Dr. Meeta Amit Burande[1] and Ms. Divya Dhanuka[2]

[1]Dr. Meeta Amit Burande
MBBS, MD Pharmacology,
Professor, Dept of Pharmacology,
D Y Patil Medical College,
Kolhapur, Maharashtra.

[2]Ms. Divya Dhanuka
Sophomore year law student
National Law School of
India University, Bangalore

Abstract

Informed consent is the integral part of any research protocol and to be prepared and obtained as per the national guidelines after the ethical committee approval. Elements and principals of consent ensure the freedom the decision after understanding the research consent and assured privacy and confidentiality. Assent, consent by Legally acceptable representative, reconsent or fresh consent all assure the same soul of informed consent. Guidelines for joint consent, vulnerable group, covid 19 or emergencies, deceptive studies as well as use of artificial intelligence is well framed to obtain the inform consent with methods other than traditional oral or written.

Definition

"Informed Consent (IC) is the decision taken freely, to take part in a research after being duly informed of its nature, significance, implications and risks, by any person capable of giving consent or, where the person is not capable of giving consent, by his or her legally acceptable representative (LAR); which must be written, signed, dated, and appropriately documented, if the concerned person is unable to write, oral or other way of consent may be given in the presence of at least one witness as per national guidelines."[1]

Requisites[4]

1. Participant should be able to give consent if not it should be by legally accepted representative i.e. LAR
2. Voluntarily obtained
3. Privacy and confidentiality should be maintained
4. Mandatory in[1]

A. Research involves Patients, children, incompetent/ incapacitated persons, healthy volunteers, immigrants, others i.e., prisoners
B. Research uses or collects Human genetic materials, biological samples, personal data

Waiver of consent[1,10]

If the research involves less than minimal risk to participants and waiver will not adversely affect the rights and welfare of the participants as well as privacy and confidentiality is maintained then waiver is scientifically justified.

For example –

- Retrospective studies, where the participants are de-identified or cannot be contacted
- Research on anonymized biological samples/ data, left over samples after clinical investigation/ research, cell lines or cell free derivatives like viral isolates, DNA or RNA from recognized institutions or qualified investigators, samples or data from repositories or registries, etc. provided permission for future research on these samples has been taken in the previous consent form
- Certain types of public health studies/ surveillance programmes/programme evaluation studies
- Research on data available in the public domain documents, records, works, performances, reviews, quality assurance studies, archival materials, or third-party interviews

Corresponding author: Dr. Meeta Amit Burande. Can be contacted at phone number+91 98509 37261.
Email id: drmeetamit@gmail.com

- Research during humanitarian emergencies and disasters, when the participant may not be in position to give consent i.e. neonatal resuscitation, life threatening emergencies with attempt to obtain the participant's consent at the earliest (*deferred/delayed consent*) In case if deferred consent is not given, participant should not be included in the research, and no further research related procedures /data collection must be done from the patient. Also, the data previously collected prior to the consent process should not be used without consent.

All research protocols are to be submitted to the Ethical Committee, and the decision for waiver of consent will be taken by EC.

Re-consent or Fresh consent[1,4,10]

As informed consent is the continuous process it is reenforced when –
- New information related to research becomes available that may change the risk benefit ratio
- Participant who was unable to understand is now able to understand the research implications i.e. regain of consciousness, insight, and mental competence
- When minor become adult i.e. 18yrs of age during the research course or LAR is changed
- Research requiring long-term follow-up or extension
- Any change in research protocol that may impact participant's decision to continue in the research i.e. change in treatment modality, procedures, site visits, data collection methods or tenure of participation
- Possible identity disclosure through data presentation or camouflaged photographs in upcoming publication
- Partner/spouse may also be needed to give additional re-consent in some cases.
- Research on stored biological sample if not anonymized.

Principals of consent[3]

- Physician or any other individual with appropriate scientific training and qualifications should seek the consent. "After ensuring that the potential subject has understood the information, the physician or another appropriately qualified individual must then seek the potential subject's freely-given informed consent."[2]
- There should be different consent for different group and separate consent for each intervention
- Once Informed consent document is approved by ethical committee, it is the part of protocol. Only EC approved version of the consent form, including its local translations should be used.
- There should be no restriction on the participant's right to ask questions related to the study or to discuss with family and friends or take time before coming to a decision
- Test of understanding may be done for sensitive studies with repeats till complete understanding of contents by participants.
- It should be bilingual or trilingual with back-to-back translated and printed to compare.
- It is Written and signed, if oral -signed by literate witness as well as by researcher or staff and One Copy is given to participant
- Community agreement may be obtained prior but does not replace IC.
- Tests that may have further implication on follow-up or treatment should be provided pre and post-test counselling relevant to the tests.

Part of consent[3]

Information sheet – it describes research and nature of participation and written in third person. It includes.

Essential components[4,10] –

1. Statement mentioning that it is research
2. Purpose and methods of the research in simple language
3. Identification of any products which are experimental[7]
4. Expected duration of the participation and frequency of contact with estimated number of participants to be enrolled, types of data collection and methods
5. Benefits to the participant, community or others that might reasonably be expected as an outcome of research
6. Any foreseeable risks, discomfort or inconvenience to the participant resulting from participation in the study
7. Extent to which confidentiality of records could be maintained, such as the limits to which the researcher would be able to safeguard confidentiality i.e. Encryption[5] and the anticipated consequences of breach of confidentiality
8. Payment/reimbursement for participation and incidental expenses depending on the type of study
9. Free treatment and/or compensation of participants for research-related injury and/ or harm
10. Freedom of the individual to participate and/or withdraw from research at any time without penalty or loss of benefits to which the participant would otherwise be entitled
11. The identity of the research team and contact persons with addresses and phone numbers for different level or type of queries.

Additional components [4]

1. Any alternative procedures or courses of treatment that might be as advantageous to the participant as the ones to which she/he is going to be subjected
2. If there is a possibility that the research could lead to any stigmatizing condition, for example HIV and genetic disorders, provision for pretest- and post-test counselling
3. Insurance coverage if any, for research-related or other adverse events

4. Foreseeable extent of information on possible current and future uses of the biological material and of the data to be generated from the research.
    A. period of storage of the sample/data and probability of the material being used for secondary purposes.
    B. whether material is to be shared with others, this should be clearly mentioned.
    C. right to prevent use of her/his biological sample, such as DNA, cell-line, etc., and related data at any time during or after the conduct of the research.
    D. risk of discovery of biologically sensitive information and provisions to safeguard confidentiality.
    E. post research plan/benefit sharing, if research on biological material and/or data leads to commercialization.
    F. Publication plan, if any, including photographs and pedigree charts.

5. Certificate of consent –it is written in first person and should include the consent of participant and witness.
A. I have read the foregoing information, or it has been read to me. I have had the opportunity to ask questions about it and any questions that I have asked have been answered to my satisfaction. I consent voluntarily to participate as a participant in this study
B. I have accurately read or witnessed the reading of the consent form to the potential participant, and the individual has had the opportunity to ask questions. I confirm that consent was given freely.

Documentation of informed consent process

Each prospective participant/LAR should sign/ thumb impressed the informed consent form after going through the informed consent process of receiving information, understanding it and voluntarily agreeing to participate in the research witnessed by an impartial literate witness along with researcher. Permission from head of institute/spouse of participant may be obtained if needed.

Essential Elements of consent[1,7]

a. A statement that the study involves research

b. An explanation of the purposes of the research
c. The expected duration of the subject's participation
d. A description of all procedures to be followed
e. Identification of any products which are experimental[7]

Informed consent in children[1]

Children are unable to sign for themselves, but should be given opportunity, whenever at all appropriate, to have their permission or concerns to be recorded as well.[3]
A LAR is an individual or judicial or other body authorized under applicable law to consent on behalf of a prospective participant to participate in research or to undergo a diagnostic, therapeutic, or preventive procedure as per research protocol[10].
The parental/LARs' permission for the child's participation in the research is termed as 'consent', whereas the child's agreement to participate is termed as 'assent'[10]
There is separate informed consent for parents/LAR and assent for children.

Children's assent[10]

The assent process should consider the children's developmental level, capability of understanding, cultural and social factors, previous experience in chronic illness.

They should be told about exactly what exactly will be happened with more practical aspect of research rather than abstract concepts.

Increase more information on research for older group in easy language and take informed consent whenever child attains the age of 18yrs.

Method of taking assent is defined as per age of child –

- Less than 7 years – LAR/Parents' consent is taken but the child is informed with the help of pictures and practical

- Between 7 to 11 years- oral assent in easy language in presence of LAR and should be countersigned by LAR for affirmation of child

- Between 12 to 18 – written informed assent to be obtained for new participant as well as if child become 12 years old during course of study

- above 18years – informed consent for new participant as well as if child become 18 years old during course of study

Child refusal should be respected and there should be no pressure for affirmation on child even from parents. They should be explained their right of refusal even later in the study. Assent should include how research may affect child's home, school, and social activities.

Waiver of assent[10]

It may be obtained in following situations from ethical committees:
1) If the research has the potential of directly benefiting the child and this benefit is available only in the research context.
2) if the research involves children with mental retardation and other developmental disabilities, where the children may not have the developmental level and intellectual capability of giving assent.
3) Assent may also be waived under the same conditions in which adult's informed consent may be waived.

Content of assent form[10]

The type and amount of information should be simplified and age-appropriate and includes -
1. What the study is about and how it might help
2. What will happen and when
3. What discomfort there might be and what will be done to minimize it
4. Who will answer the child's questions during the study
5. Whether an option to say "no" exists

Consent of parent/LAR[10]

Generally informed consent of one parent/LAR in low-risk studies and both parents in high-risk studies is obtained but ethical committee determine the whether consent of one or both parents is to be taken. One parent consent is sufficient if ONLY he/she is responsible for child care.

It should include information about growth and development, psychological well-being, and school attendance of child, in addition to all components of information sheet. Cognitively impaired and mental retarded children and their parents are the vulnerable populations and to be explained very carefully due to likelihood of misunderstandings.

Waiver of parent/LAR consent[10]

EC may waive parental/LAR consent and instruct to safeguard the interest of the child, If research involves sensitive issues like neglect and abuse of a child.

Informed consent in Incapacitated adults/vulnerable group[1]

"The interests of the patient always prevail over those of science and society"

Vulnerable persons like mentally-deficient persons, severely-injured patients – should be excluded as much as possible. Consent is obtained from legal accepted representative if –

- Consent represents the subject's presumed will.
- The person not able to give informed legal consent has received information according to his/her capacity of understanding.
- The research is essential to validate data obtained in clinical trials on persons able to give informed consent or by other research methods.
- The research relates directly to a life-threatening or debilitating clinical condition from which the incapacitated adult concerned suffers.
- There are grounds for expecting that administering the medicinal product to be all.

tested will produce a benefit to the patient outweighing the risks or produce no risk at

- Socially, economically, or politically disadvantaged individuals who are susceptible to being exploited
- Terminally ill patients ready to consent in search of new interventions.
- In case of differently abled participants, such as individuals with physical, neurological or mental disabilities, appropriate measures should be taken to increase participants' understanding, i.e. braille for the visually impaired.

Informed consent in Illiterate population[1]

To obtain informed consent from illiterate individual involved in trial/research following strategies should be used: -

- Presence of a community representative trained by the scientific team.
- Witnessing the oral approval by a trained and independent community representative.
- Community representative will verify that the purpose of the research has been explained to the participant till it is well understood.

Gatekeepers

Gatekeeper is head/leader of the group or culturally appropriate authority. Witnessed permission of gatekeeper may be obtained in writing or recorded audio/video on behalf of the group.

Community consent

Community consent is required if participants cannot participate unless the community's consent is available or individual consent cannot be taken due to risk of change in behaviour. Here community representee committee i.e. village panchayat, give permission with full quorum along with seeking of individual consent.

Consent for studies using deception[5]

Some research studies i.e. psychology or the

behavioural sciences, require deception due to nature of research design when there is no other non-deceptive way of investigating the research problem. Here true informed consent may cause modification and may defeat the purpose of research, hence difficult to obtain at initiation.

So, 2 step approach may be practiced –
- Step1 - initial consent about the nature of the study along with scientific aim in full
- Step2 - detailed information with explanation of deception as early as possible preferable just after participation and certainly no later than all data collection; choice of withdrawing their data should be informed.

Unjustified deception, intimidation, and undue influence to be avoided. Approval from EC is needed before implementation ensuring that the study does not involve the possibility of participants suffering any degree of pain or substantial emotional distress.

Informed consent in multicentric research

Joint consent will be minimum consent with addition as per local circumstances. Informed consent document[11] should clearly mention that the study is a part of the multicentre study and is prepared in a simplified manner. If many languages, original consent will be in researchers' language. It may include audio/visual/other advocacy materials to improve the understanding of participants. Local centre should incorporate site specific modifications as per local needs and should provide the copy of their consent too[3.] It should be backed with English translation and certificate of consent. Overall content of Informed Consent Document should be uniform. Identity of research team, contact address as well as measures for privacy and confidentiality should be ensured across all the study centres. MoU between the participating centres and Coordinating Centre may obtained if needed. There should be clear protocol for data sharing, custodianship, and maintenance/storage etc.

Informed consent in research involving imaging procedures[1]

- Type of exposure (intensity, duration, eventual repetition) and on the eventual long-term effects.
- Use of contrast fluid and the eventual toxicity.
- patient/volunteer's medical information: previous treatments, presence of implants, asthma, allergy, renal failure, hypertension, claustrophobia.

Informed consent in genetic research

Other family members may be involved as *Secondary Informed Consent Process Participants* if family history is recorded including their identifiable details and their informed consent will also be needed.

Informed consent in covid[9]-

To obtain valid informed consent in COVID-19 is a challenge due to practical difficulties in reaching out to a patient - COVID ward, isolation or quarantine and very low decisional capacity to differentiate between guidelines and research. Covid 19 patients are vulnerable of being stigmatized due to contagious spread and imposed risk to staff as well as contacts.

Informed consent is prepared as Electronic Consent to avoid direct interaction with the patient in isolation. Technology and electronic tools are to be used to prepare interactive formats, text, graphics, podcasts, audio, video, interactive website, platforms to explain information related to a study. Informed assent/consent is documented electronically by digital signature, audio video recording etc. Online consent also may be obtained.

Artificial intelligence in consent[12]

- Research participants must understand the alternatives available for the AI technology in question, including traditional methods/ doing nothing/comparable risk -benefits.

- Participant must understand the process and must evaluate the research subject by any evaluation technique i.e. "teach-back", or "show-me" with ongoing education and multiple time consents.
- Stakeholder should be clear about role of human caregivers and technology and clearly explained to the participant.
- Possibility of missteps and risk attached to it should be clearly explained.
- AI technology should not make the value judgements on people behalf.

Procedures after the consent process

After consent is obtained, the participant should be given a copy of same. Any deviation should be recorded. The original PIS and ICF should be archived as per protocol guidelines.

Concerns regarding informed consent[10]

Obtaining informed consent/assent should not be a mere formality to obtain participants' signatures on the forms. It should be a process, to ensure that participant understand what is going on in the research with opportunities to ask questions. The consent process is ongoing interaction between researcher and participant, to help resolve the queries that may arise during the study. The language should be simple and easy to understand with avoidance of medical and technical terms. To avoid *therapeutic misconception*, participant should clearly understand that participation is in research and purpose of research differs from normal clinical care i.e. to generate knowledge for future.

Responsibility of researchers[4]

1researcher should ensure that informed consent is taken as per guidelines after EC approval and no deviation from protocol is there including in the process of obtaining the consent as well as during and after the study. Refusal to give informed consent by participant should not affect the clinical patient doctor relationship or routine care of participant.

Some legal battles on Informed Consent

Ram Bihari Lal v. Dr JN Shrivastava,[13] The doctor performed an operation on a patient with appendicitis after obtaining proper consent. However, during the surgery, it was found that the patient's appendix was not inflamed but instead the gallbladder was gangrenous. Surgeon removed the gallbladder in same operation. Patient has dies after 3 days due to hepatorenal syndrome probably due to prolonged anaesthesia. The court held the doctor responsible for operating without consent and emphasized that while a medical professional may act in the patient's best interest, the law prioritizes an individual's dignity, autonomy, and their right to decide about themselves.

Samira Kohli v Dr Prabha Manchanda,[14] explicitly lays out the court's stance on informed consent in medical practice. Patient, a 44 years old unmarried woman was having DUB and advised diagnostic laparoscopy with need of laparotomy under General anesthesia as informed for consent with USG report of fibroid or suspected endometriosis. However, during the procedure, the patient was unconscious, so her mother was consulted to provide consent for a hysterectomy with bilateral removal of tubes and ovary in view of grade 4 endometriosis. This consent was considered a proxy consent. The court ruled in favor of the patient, stating that the removal of her reproductive organ was carried out without her genuine consent even if it was in favor of patient, it was not emergency life threatening. Consequently, the doctor in this case was held responsible for the same.

And lastly, In the case of **Satishchandra Shukla,**[15] the case was filed against PHC doctor and nurse for performing vasectomy on a satishchandra who was illeterate, not medically sound and unmarried. Details revealed that in consent he has informed the nurse that he is married and has two female children. His father claimed that patient was of unsound mind and it will affect his future marriage and security in life. Case was dismissed saying patient has voluntarily came to hospital to get the operation done with motive of receiving money and well aware of the consequence and not incapable enough to give consent.

Conclusion

The basics of consent rely upon whether it is implied, expressed or informed. It is necessary to distinguish and follow the procedure even when acting in the best interest of the patient to mitigate any such legal injury and thoroughly avoid any medical negligence in this affair.

Informed Consent (IC) is a continuous process involving three main components –relevant information, competence of participant, and assuring voluntariness of participation. Individual's freedom of choice and autonomy[4] is protected by Informed voluntary consent.

Samples of consent are available at the references quoted [5,6,8]

References:

1. https://ec.europa.eu/research/participants/data/ref/fp7/89807/informed-consent_en.pdf
2. World Medical Association Declaration of Helsinki. Ethical Principles for Medical Research Involving Human Subjects. Available from: http://www.wma.net
3. https://cdn.who.int/media/docs/default-source/documents/ethics/informed-decision-making.pdf?sfvrsn=8b3cf04f_0
4. **https://main.icmr.nic.in/sites/default/files/guidelines/ICMR_Ethical_Guidelines_2017.pdf**
5. https://info.lse.ac.uk/staff/services/Policies-and-procedures/Assets/Documents/infCon.pdf
6. https://medicine.hofstra.edu/pdf/research/sample-informed-consent-form-for-hofstra-irb-proposal.pdf
7. https://www.compliance.iastate.edu/sites/default/files/imported/irb/forms/docs/consent-elements.pdf
8. https://main.icmr.nic.in/sites/default/files/forms/Common_Forms.pdf
9. https://main.icmr.nic.in/sites/default/files/guidelines/EC_Guidance_COVID19_06_05_2020.pdf
10. https://main.icmr.nic.in/sites/default/files/guidelines/National_Ethical_Guidelines_for_BioMedical_Research_Involving_Children_0.pdf
11. https://main.icmr.nic.in/sites/default/files/guidelines/FINAL_Joint_Ethics_Review_17032023.pdf
12. https://main.icmr.nic.in/sites/default/files/upload_documents/Ethical_Guidelines_AI_Healthcare_2023.pdf
13. Ram Bihari Lal v. Dr. J. N. Srivastava, AIR 1985 MP 150
14. v Samira Kohli v. Dr. Prabha Manchanda and Anr., 2008, (1) SCALE 442
15. Satishchandra Shukla vs Union of India, 1 (1986) ACC 46.

Chapter 14

Responsibility and Common Challenges of Sponsors in Clinical Trial

Dr. Prajak Barde[1*], Ms. Monali Shende[2], Ms. Varsha Shitole[3], Dr. Mohini Barde[4]

[1]Dr. Prajak Barde
Founder and CMO, Med Indite Communications Pvt Ltd, Manjri, Pune. 412307

[2]Ms. Monali Shende
Executive, Clinical Research and Development, Med Indite Communications Pvt Ltd, Manjri, Pune. 412307

[3]Ms. Varsha Shitole
Executive, Clinical Research and Development, Med Indite Communications Pvt Ltd, Manjri, Pune. 412307

[4]Dr. Mohini Barde
Founder and Managing Director, Med Indite Communications Pvt Ltd, Manjri, Pune. 412307

Abstract

The objective of this brief review is to give an overall understanding of the responsibilities of the sponsor in a clinical trial setting and to discuss the common challenges that the sponsor encounters and their probable solutions. The **sponsor** in the clinical studies can be an individual, company, institution, or organization that takes responsibility for the initiation, management, and/or financing of a clinical trial, and is entrusted with the responsibility of conducting the study in accordance with the protocol, Good Clinical Practice (GCP), and applicable regulatory requirements and ensuring the protection of study participants and the reliability of trial results. The sponsor should ensure the protection of study participants and the reliability of trial results. By working with experienced partners, utilizing innovative technologies, and prioritizing patient engagement, sponsors can overcome these challenges and drive successful clinical trials. Please read the complete article for knowing more.

The objective of this brief review is to give an overall understanding of the responsibilities of the sponsor in a clinical trial setting and to discuss the common challenges that the sponsor encounters and their probable solutions. The **sponsor** in the clinical studies can be an individual, company, institution, or organization that takes responsibility for the initiation, management, and/or financing of a clinical trial, and is entrusted with the responsibility of conducting the study in accordance with the protocol, Good Clinical Practice (GCP), and applicable regulatory requirements and ensuring the protection of study participants and the reliability of trial results. [1]

Sponsor responsibilities are very broad, encompassing end-to-end clinical trial-related activities. As per the ICH-GCP, NDCTR 2019 guidelines, the key responsibilities of the sponsor include developing study documents (e.g., protocol, case report form

Corresponding author: Dr. Prajak Barde. Can be contacted at phone number+91 99665 77785.
Email id: drprajaktb@medindite.com

[CRF], informed consent form [ICF], etc.), implementing and maintaining quality assurance and quality control process, trial management, data handling, and record-keeping, notification and/or approval of the proposal to the competent regulatory authority(ies), confirmation of review by the Institutional Review Board (IRB)/Independent Ethics Committee (IEC), handling of the investigational product (manufacturing, packaging, labelling, supplying and handling the investigational product(s)) as per the good laboratory practices (GLP) as appropriate, funding and budget management, monitoring and oversight, safety reporting, audit, and preparation of study report.[2] The sponsor can delegate these study-related duties and responsibilities to the respective identified person(s) /organization(s), known as Contract Research Organisation (CRO), however, all responsibility always lies with the sponsor. The sponsor selects well-qualified, trained, and experienced investigator(s) for the conduct of the trial for the entire duration of the study. Standard operating procedures should be documented by Sponsor to ensure compliance with Good Clinical Practices Guidelines and applicable regulations.

In this endeavour, the sponsor may face various problems in clinical trials such as the development of the protocol, the selection of a study site, a lack of funding to complete a trial, safety reporting, and monitoring, as well as issues with patient recruitment, enrollment, and retention.[3]

While developing the study protocol, it is important that the study should be well-planned, and appropriately justified based on the available pre-clinical/clinical data, scientifically designed to evaluate the hypothesis in question, and at the same time, the procedure/end points and other safety and efficacy tools listed in the protocol ensures the protection of study participants and the reliability of trial results. Therefore, the sponsor needs to collaborate with multiple stakeholders including subject matter experts and ensure that all elements of the protocol as given in ICH-E6, local ethical and regulatory requirements are taken care of. Final study protocol should have scientific and operational rigor and should carefully agree to by all contributors and collaborators, and the precise roles of each team member should be explained. The sponsor should pay special attention to vulnerable patients to avoid breaches of ethical codes (e.g., children, prisoners, pregnant women, mentally challenged, educationally and economically disadvantaged).[4]

The sponsor is responsible for the study site selection and is an important aspect of the clinical trial process. Poor choices can lead directly to poor patient accrual and study failure, or to a costly exercise of including additional study sites or protocol amendment. This challenge may be encountered by the sponsor during the recruitment of patients, often most intensely in rare diseases and in pediatric trials. Recruitment for such trials is often difficult and costly, sometimes with only one or two patients enrolled per study site. Given the significant resources required to develop rare disease treatments, study sponsors are well-positioned to ensure sufficient recruitment for the study and to assist sites with the recruitment of subjects.[5] The recruitment can be improved by optimizing communication/advertising to maximize cost-effectiveness and targeting communication to meet the patient profile.

When possible, having contingency plans to open additional sites, perform extra recruitment, and cover protocol amendments is recommended. To minimize study site failure, the sponsor needs to know the site history, staff experience, investigator enthusiasm, available population, expected patient burden, and financial impact.[3]

The funding and budget management should be provided by the sponsor as trials can be failed due to lack of funding. For example, Hwang *et al.* [6] noted that 22% of the failed phase 3 studies they examined failed due to lack of funding.

Another challenge is documentation, many sponsors make the mistake of not documenting their oversight checks. A lack of documentation can put a sponsor at risk of non-compliance as well as cast doubt on the clinical data generated. Managing clinical trials takes a great deal of work and involves many people and processes. Documentation of quality checks and findings will help ensure that mistakes are not repeated and the data from the trial are reliable. Sponsors should invest time in high-quality documentation.[7]

Sponsors also have challenges in safety reporting, monitoring, and clinical trial supplies management of the clinical trial as happened during the COVID-19 pandemic. The sponsor must comply with the safety reporting timeline and submit the reports of the serious adverse event, after due analysis, within stipulated timelines. During the pandemic, this was done via e-mail with electronic signatures as per the Central Drugs Standards Control Organization (CDSCO). Digital submissions were also acceptable by the regulatory authorities in the wake of the pandemic.[8] Similarly, the planned on-site monitoring visits were not possible during the COVID-19 pandemic leading to delays in on-site monitoring (source data verification) that may result in delayed identification of major protocol deviations, or nonreporting of SAEs, etc.[9] In such a situation, alternative approaches such as enhanced central monitoring/risk-based monitoring, telephonic contact with the sites to review study procedures, trial participant status, or remote monitoring of enrolled trial participants, were implemented, where appropriate and feasible. In the case of Investigational Medicinal Product (IMP) supplies during the pandemic, the sponsor provided an uninterrupted supply of the investigational product to the patients, e.g., distributing the investigational products direct to the patient through a courier service.[10]

Utilizing key technology tools such as electronic case report forms (eCRF), electronic data capture (EDC), and electronic trial master files (eTMF) or digital diaries have provided access to and review regularly the data contained within the system(s) and help with documentation of sponsor clinical trial oversight through an audit trail.[7]

Conclusion:

The sponsor's role is key to the success of clinical trials. The sponsor should ensure that the study is conducted in accordance with the protocol, GCP, and applicable regulatory requirements. The sponsor should ensure the protection of study participants and the reliability of trial results. By working with experienced partners, utilizing innovative technologies, and prioritizing patient engagement, sponsors can overcome these challenges and drive successful clinical trials.

References:

1. Ray S, and others (eds), Role and responsibilities of the sponsor. *Oxford Handbook of Clinical and Healthcare Research*, 1, Oxford Medical Handbooks (Oxford, 2016; online edn, Oxford Academic, 1 Mar. 2016).

2. Integrated Addendum to ICH E6(R1): Guideline for Good Clinical Practice E6(R2), Current Step 4 version dated: 9 November 2016. Guidance for Industry: E6(R2) Good Clinical Practice: Integrated Addendum to ICH E6(R1) (fda.gov).

3. Fogel DB. Factors associated with clinical trials that fail and opportunities for improving the likelihood of success: A review. Contemp Clin Trials Commun. 2018 Aug 7; 11:156-164.

4. Jenn NC. Common ethical issues in Research and Publication. Malays Fam Physician. 2006 Aug 31;1(2-3):74-6.

5. U.S. Department Health and Human Services. Attachment B - New Challenges in Interactions among Sponsors, Clinical Trial Sites, and Study Subjects. SACHRP Recommendation.https://www.hhs.gov/ohrp/sachrpcommittee/recommendations/attachment-b-new-challenges-sponsor-clinical-trial-site-subject.html.

6. Hwang TJ, Carpenter D, Lauffenburger JC, *et al.* Failure of investigational drugs in late-stage clinical development and publication of trial results. *JAMA Intern. Med.* 2016; 176:1826–1833.

7. The Importance of Sponsor Oversight in Clinical Trials. 2021. https://sureclinical.com/2021/06/30/the-importance-of-sponsor-oversight-in-clinical-trials/.

8. Office Circular Issued by CDSCO dated. Regarding Conduct of clinical Trial during Special Situation Due to Outbreak of COVID-19; 30 March 2020.

9. FDA Guidance on Conduct of Clinical Trials of Medical Products during COVID-19 Public Health Emergency. Guidance for Industry, Investigators, and Institutional Review Boards; Edition March 2020 updated on 02 June 2020. Available from: https://www.fda.gov/regulatory-information/search-fda-guidance-documents. [Last accessed on 2020 Jun 01.

10. Davis S, Pai S. Challenges and opportunities for sponsors in conducting clinical trials during a pandemic. Perspect Clin Res. 2020;11(3):115-120.

Chapter 15

Safety reporting and Pharmacovigilance in Clinical Trials

Dr. Akash Gadgade[1] and Dr. Jyothsna C S[2]

[1]Dr. Akash Gadgade
MBBS, MD Pharmacology,
Associate Director,
Medical & Scientific Affairs,
Navitas Life Sciences, Bengaluru,
Karnataka

[2]Dr. Jyothsna C S,

MBBS, MD Pharmacology,

Medical Advisor , Pfizer, India

Abstract

ADR is a response to a drug that is 'noxious, unintended and occurs at doses normally used in man'. The incidence of ADRs has remained relatively unchanged over time; with research suggesting that between 5% and 10% of patients may suffer from an ADR at admission, during admission or at discharge, despite various preventative efforts. In this article, definitions and importance of ADRs reporting, Pharamcovigilance, ICSR, PSUR, DSUR, PBRER etc, ADRs, SAEs, CT Safety reporting requirements/ Timelines are discussed briefly.

Adverse Drug Reaction

The most commonly used definition of an ADR is a response to a drug that is 'noxious, unintended and occurs at doses normally used in man'. This definition arose from the World Health Organization (WHO) report on International Drug Monitoring in 1972, and remains largely unchanged. Since 2012, the definition has included reactions occurring as a result of error, misuse or abuse, and to suspect reactions to medicines that are unlicensed or being used off-label in addition to the authorised use of a medicinal product in normal doses. While this change potentially alters the reporting and surveillance carried out by manufactures and medicines regulators, in clinical practice it should not affect our approach to managing ADRs. The incidence of ADRs has remained relatively unchanged over time; with research suggesting that between 5% and 10% of patients may suffer from an ADR at admission, during admission or at discharge, despite various preventative efforts.

Drug reactions can be classified into immunologic and non-immunologic etiologies. The majority (75 to 80 percent) of adverse drug reactions are caused by predictable, non-immunologic effects.

Corresponding author: Dr. Akash Gadgade. Can be contacted at phone number+91 98452 25122.
Email id: drakashgadgade@gmail.com

The remaining 20 to 25 percent of adverse drug events are caused by unpredictable effects that may or may not be immune mediated. Immune-mediated reactions account for 5 to 10 percent of all drug reactions and constitute true drug hypersensitivity, with IgE-mediated drug allergies falling into this category.

The Gell and Coombs classification system describes the predominant immune mechanisms that lead to clinical symptoms of drug hypersensitivity. This classification system includes: Type I reactions (IgE-mediated); Type II reactions (cytotoxic); Type III reactions (immune complex); and Type IV reactions (delayed, cell-mediated). However, some drug hypersensitivity reactions are difficult to classify because of a lack of evidence supporting a predominant immunologic mechanism. These include certain cutaneous drug reactions (i.e., maculopapular rashes, erythroderma, exfoliative dermatitis, and fixed drug reactions) and specific drug hypersensitivity syndromes.

Pharmacovigilance

"The science and activities relating to the detection, assessment, understanding and prevention of adverse effects or any other drug-related problem."It is an essential component of patient care and rational use of medicines. It is also variously referred to as adverse drug reaction monitoring, drug safety surveillance, side effect monitoring, spontaneous reporting, post-marketing surveillance or variations of these.

Pharmacovigilance involves the safety monitoring of all medicines including herbal and complementary remedies, vaccines and biological substances.
Whilst all pharmaceuticals including biological tend to demonstrate side effects, most of which have been extensively researched on, there continue to remain several side effects that are hidden or undisclosed for years after marketing the drug. Therefore, maintaining strict surveillance of all side effects, both known as well as unknown, becomes crucial in the process of gaining new information and data with regards to the drug safety profile

Pharmacovigilance programme of India

National Pharmacovigilance Programme of India, was inaugurated on23rd November 2004 and became operational on 1st January 2005. The setup of the programme comprised of two zonal centres i.e. the South West centre in Mumbai, which further had three regional centres and the North-East centre in New Delhi, which further had 2 regional centres. Each regional centre was further provided with several peripheral centres (24 in total). Unfortunately, the World Bank funding for this programme ended in mid-2009 and this programme was temporarily suspended. Recognising the establishment of a strong Pharmacovigilance system as the need of the hour, the Department of Pharmacology, AIIMS and the CDSCO, under the aegis of the Ministry of Health and Family Welfare (MHFW), together, put forward the framework for a new and improved program in 2009. This program was christened as the Pharmacovigilance Programme of India (PVPI) and was inaugurated on 14th July 2010. In order to better implement this programme, the National Coordination Centre (NCC) was shifted from AIIMS, New Delhi to Indian Pharmacopoeia Commission (IPC), Ghaziabad, in April 2011.The primary aim of the NCC at the IPC is to generate safety data on medicines as per the global drug safety monitoring standards.

Adverse Drug Reaction Data Flow

ADR reports submitted at the Adverse Drug Monitoring Centre(AMC's) will be subjected to an initial check by the PV staff. These ADR forms are then forwarded to the coordinating centres and the AMC staff will keep a log of all the activities carried out. On receiving the ADR forms, the coordinating centre will conduct a causality assessment prior to uploading the reports onto the PV database. A consolidated report of ADR's will be collected at predefined time intervals by the coordinating centre. The integrated data will then be transmitted through VigiFlow interface into the Uppsala Monitoring Centre (UMC) ADR database and signal processing will be carried out.

The establishment of relationship between medicine intake and occurrence of adverse events is an important activity in pharmacovigilance. Different national pharmacovigilance centres have different procedures for carrying out case causality assessment, driven sometimes by differing philosophies on the need for and importance of case causality assessment.

ICSR

A spontaneous report is an unsolicited communication by health care professionals or consumers that describes one or more ADRs in a patient who was given one or more medicinal products and that does not derive from a study or any organized data collection scheme. A new term has been introduced that will supplant the use of 'spontaneous reports'. This is 'individual case safety reports (ICSR)'. ICSRs play a major role in the identification of signals of risk once a medicine is marketed. ICSRs can also provide important information on at-risk groups, risk factors (to a limited degree), and clinical features of known serious ADRs. Spontaneous reporting is dependent on clinicians and other health professionals who need to be trained and encouraged to report details of suspected adverse reactions in patients on ARV treatment. Under-reporting is a serious problem with this method, but reporting can be intensified in selected units e.g. hospitals.

PSUR

Periodic safety update reports (PSURs) are pharmacovigilance documents intended to provide an evaluation of the risk-benefit balance of a medicinal product for submission by marketing authorisation holders at defined time points during the post-authorisation phase. The objective of the PSUR is to present a comprehensive and critical analysis of the risk-benefit balance of the product, taking into account new or emerging safety information in the context of cumulative information on risk and benefits.

As per the requirements of Schedule "Y" of the Drugs and Cosmetics Rules, Periodic Safety Update Reports (PSURS) of new drugs are required to be submitted to the office of DCGI every six months for the first two years and for subsequent two years; the PSUR shall be submitted annually.

DSUR

The development safety update report (DSUR) is pre-marketing periodic report which covers safety information of drugs, biological, vaccines and combo products under development (including marketed drugs that are under further study) among the ICH regions. A single DSUR including safety data from all clinical trials conducted with the drug should be prepared for an investigational drug.

The main objective of a DSUR is to present a comprehensive, thoughtful annual review and evaluation of pertinent safety information collected during the reporting period related to a drug under investigation, whether or not it is marketed, examining whether the information obtained by the sponsor during the reporting period is in accord with previous knowledge of the investigational drug's safety and describing new safety issues that could have an impact on the protection of clinical trial subjects. It summarizes the current understanding and management of identified and potential risks providing an update on the status of the clinical investigation/development program and study results.

PBRER

The main objective of a Periodic Benefit-Risk Evaluation Report (PBRER) is to present a comprehensive, concise, and critical analysis of new or emerging information on the risks of the medicinal product, and on its benefit in approved indications, to enable an appraisal of the product's overall benefit-risk profile.

SUSAR

Suspected unexpected serious adverse reaction is used to refer to an adverse event that occurs in a clinical trial subject, which is assessed by the sponsor and/or study investigator as being unexpected, serious and as having a reasonable possibility of a causal relationship with the study drug. Seriousness criteria have been stated above. Any event which would have led to one of the consequences that fulfil serious criteria but did not, owing to timely medical intervention, may also be deemed a suspected unexpected serious adverse reaction. Such reactions are to be submitted in an expedited manner to the sponsor, Institutional Ethics Committee (IEC), and regulatory authority. The investigator should report SUSAR within 48 hours of occurrence.

SAE

According to the The New Drugs and Clinical Trials Rules, 2019, a "serious adverse event" (SAE) means an untoward medical occurrence during clinical trial resulting in death or permanent disability, or hospitalisation of the trial subject where the trial subject is an outdoor patient or a healthy person, prolongation of hospitalisation where the trial subject is an indoor-patient, persistent or significant disability or incapacity, congenital anomaly, birth defect or life threatening event.

Clinical Trial Safety reporting requirements/ timelines

The New Drugs and Clinical Trials Rules mandates that the investigator shall report all serious adverse events to the Central Licensing Authority, the sponsor or its representative, who has obtained permission from the Central Licensing Authority for conduct of clinical trial or bioavailability or bioequivalence study, as the case may be, and the Ethics Committee that accorded approval to the study protocol, within twenty-four hours of their occurrence. If the investigator fails to report any serious adverse event within the stipulated period, he shall have to furnish the reasons for delay to the satisfaction of the Central Licensing Authority along with the report of the serious adverse event. For a BA/BE study, any report of serious adverse event should be forwarded to Central Licensing Authority within fourteen days of its occurrence.

Timeline of Safety Reporting of Serious Adverse Events is presented in Figure No. 01.

Data Safety Monitoring Board

DSMB is a group of individuals with pertinent experience that reviews on a regular basis the accumulating data from a clinical trial. It is usually appointed by the sponsor. It advises the sponsor regarding the continuing safety of trial subjects and those yet to be recruited in the trial as well as continuing validity and scientific merit of the trial. A fundamental reason to establish DSMB is to enhance the safety of trial subject in situations where safety concerns may be unusually high eg prior information suggesting possibility of serious toxicity with the study treatment.

References:

1. Patton K, Borshoff DC. Adverse drug reactions. Anaesthesia. 2018 Jan;73 Suppl 1:76-84. doi: 10.1111/anae.14143. PMID: 29313907.
2. Coleman JJ, Pontefract SK. Adverse drug reactions. Clin Med (Lond). 2016 Oct;16(5):481-485. doi: 10.7861/clinmedicine.16-5-481. PMID: 27697815; PMCID: PMC6297296.
3. Nayak S, Acharjya B. Adverse cutaneous drug reaction. Indian J Dermatol. 2008 Jan;53(1):2-8. doi: 10.4103/0019-5154.39732. PMID: 19967009; PMCID: PMC2784579.
4. Riedl MA, Casillas AM. Adverse drug reactions: types and treatment options. Am Fam Physician. 2003 Nov 1;68(9):1781-90. PMID: 14620598.
5. Suke SG, Kosta P, Negi H. Role of Pharmacovigilance in India: An overview. Online J Public Health Inform. 2015 Jul 1;7(2):e223. doi: 10.5210/ojphi.v7i2.5595. PMID: 26392851; PMCID: PMC4576445.
6. WHO guidelines on safety monitoring of herbal medicines in pharmacovigilance systems. Available from: https://apps.who.int/iris/bitstream/handle/10665/43034/9241592214_eng.pdf
7. Lihite RJ, Lahkar M. An update on the Pharmacovigilance Programme of India. Front Pharmacol. 2015 Sep 22;6:194. doi: 10.3389/fphar.2015.00194. PMID: 26441651; PMCID: PMC4585088.

Figure No. 01: **Timeline of Safety Reporting of Serious Adverse Events**

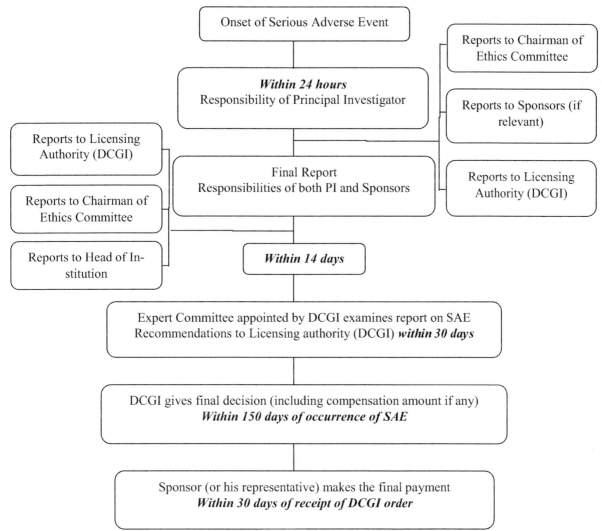

8. Kalaiselvan V, Kumar P, Mishra P, Singh GN. System of adverse drug reactions reporting: What, where, how, and whom to report? Indian J Crit Care Med. 2015 Sep;19(9):564-6. doi: 10.4103/0972-5229.164819. PMID: 26430348; PMCID: PMC4578206.

9. Sahu RK, Yadav R, Prasad P, Roy A, Chandrakar S. Adverse drug reactions monitoring: prospects and impending challenges for pharmacovigilance. Springerplus. 2014 Nov 26;3:695. doi: 10.1186/2193-1801-3-695. PMID: 25520913; PMCID: PMC4258196.

10. PV resources. Data. World Health Organization Available from: https://whopvresources.org/datainpv.php

11. A Practical Handbook on The Pharmacovigilance of Medicines Used in the Treatment of Tuberculosis: Enhancing the Safety of the Tb Patient. World Health Organization. Available from: https://www.who.int/docs/default-source/documents/tuberculosis/a-practical-handbook-on-the-pharmacovigilance-of-medicines-used-in-the-treatment-of-tuberculosis.pdf?sfvrsn=6e5fc0cf_5

12. Periodic safety update reports (PSURs). European Medicines Agency. Available from: https://www.ema.europa.eu/en/human-regulatory/post-authorisation/pharmacovigilance/periodic-safety-update-reports-psurs

13. Guideline on good pharmacovigilance practices (GVP). Module VII – Periodic safety update report (Rev 1). European Medicines Agency. Available from: https://www.ema.europa.eu/en/documents/scientific-guideline/guideline-good-pharmacovigilance-practices-gvp-module-vii-periodic-safety-update-report_en.pdf

14. Central Drug Standards Control Organization. Available from: https://cdsco.gov.in/opencms/resources/UploadCDSCOWeb/2018/UploadNewsFiles/Submission%20of%20PSUR.pdf

15. Guidance for Industry. E2F Development Safety Update Report. Available from: https://www.fda.gov/files/drugs/published/E2F-Development-Safety-Update-Report.pdf

16. ICH Topic. E2F Development Safety Update Report. European Medicines Agency. Available from: https://www.ema.europa.eu/en/documents/scientific-guideline/ich-e-2-f-development-safety-update-report-step-3_en.pdf

17. ICH guideline E2C (R2) on periodic benefit-risk evaluation report (PBRER). European Medicines Agency. Available from: https://www.ema.europa.eu/en/documents/regulatory-procedural-guideline/international-conference-harmonisation-technical-requirements-registration-pharmaceuticals-human-use_en-0.pdf

18. Sil A, Das NK. Ethics of Safety Reporting of a Clinical Trial. Indian J Dermatol. 2017 Jul-Aug;62(4):387-391. doi: 10.4103/ijd.IJD_273_17. PMID: 28794549; PMCID: PMC5527719.

19. The New Drugs and Clinical Trial Rules 2019. Central Drug Standards Control Organization. 2019.

20. Singh N, Madkaikar NJ, Gokhale PM, Parmar DV. New drugs and clinical trials rules 2019: Changes in responsibilities of the ethics committee. Perspect Clin Res. 2020 Jan-Mar;11(1):37-43. doi: 10.4103/picr.PICR_208_19. Epub 2020 Jan 31. PMID: 32154148; PMCID: PMC7034142.

21. Yao B, Zhu L, Jiang Q, Xia HA. Safety monitoring in clinical trials. Pharmaceutics. 2013 Jan 17;5(1):94-106. doi: 10.3390/pharmaceutics5010094. PMID: 24300399; PMCID: PMC3834937.

Chapter 16

Review of safety documents by regulators/ ethics committees and compensation for SAEs/Deaths as per Indian gazette notifications/ clinical trial rules.

Dr. Abhijit Munshi B.A.M.S. M.D. (in Alternative Medicine),
Director –Clinical Operations & Academics,
Alchemy Clinical Research Services,
and Ethics Committee Trainer /
Consultant. Nagpur, Maharashtra.

Abstract

Serious adverse event (SAE) is a major area of concern in Clinical Research. It is the responsibility of the investigator to provide medical care of the trial participant in all trial-related injuries and SAE and to report the event to all the stakeholders of the clinical trial. The trial sponsor is responsible for the ongoing safety evaluation of the investigational product, reporting of AE and SAE and compensation to the participant in case of any trial related SAE or Death. Monitoring and upholding the ethical principles of beneficence, justice, non-maleficence in such cases is the responsibility of the Ethics Committee and regulatory body. Adverse drug reaction (ADR) refers to any unwanted and noxious effect of a medicine when used in recommended dosages, whereas the same will be termed as an adverse event (AE) if a causal relationship is not yet established. Any AE or ADR which may results in death, in-patient hospitalization, an extension of hospitalization, persistent or significant disability or incapability, a congenital anomaly, or is else life-threatening is called an SAE. The principal investigator should report the event to the DCGI, sponsor and the Ethics Committee (EC) within 24 hours of the occurrence of the SAE. A detailed report is then submitted by both the investigator and the EC to the DCGI. And after due analysis, DCGI gives a final decision on the quantum of compensation to be paid by the sponsor to the nominee.

Introduction

Safety of the trial participant is the utmost important part of clinical trials. SAE is any untoward medical occurrence, which results in death, is life-threatening, requires inpatient hospitalization or prolongation of existing hospitalization, results in persistent or significant disability/incapacity, or is a congenital anomaly/birth defect.[1] Reporting of any SAE is the shared responsibility of all the stakeholders in a clinical trial, the PI and sponsor to the Institutional Ethics Committee (IEC) as well as the regulatory authority (Drugs Controller General of India [DCGI]) within specified timelines as per the regulations (New drug and clinical trial rule 2019).[2]

SAE reporting has become the main responsibility, particularly for clinical trial sites, as the entire focus of the Indian regulations is on the safety of human clinical trial participants.[3] After analysing and confirming the reports received by the Investigators, IEC shall recommend compensation for any trial-related death/injury [4] and provide the opinion to the DCGI on both, the causal relationship of the SAE to the investigational product and the quantum of compensation to be given to the participant within 30 days.[5]

Compensation in Clinical Trials:

Corresponding author: **Dr. Abhijit Munshi.** Can be contacted at phone number+91 9404826895
Email id: drabhijit@alchemyclinical.in

- Any monitory or other benefits received by the participants for their participation in the clinical trial; **or**
- Receipt of payment or other services in case of any trial-related injury.

Compensation is more common in Phase I trials with healthy volunteers and is paid to participants in recognition of their time sacrifice and as an appreciation of their contribution to science.[6]

Reimbursement
- Refers to any expenses incurred during the participation in a clinical trial.
- Payable to all enrolled trial participants or their legally designated representatives.
- This is documented well before a clinical trial initiation and may cover:
  - travel expenses of the trial participants,
  - accommodation,
  - Hospitalisation,
  - loss of wages,
  - food expenses.

Legislation
New drug and clinical trial rule 2019, Chapter VI and the Seventh Schedule.

The rule state that compensation is applicable to the trial participants in case of any trial related injury or death due to any of the following reason:
a. Adverse effect of the investigational product (s) (IP).
b. Protocol violation, trial misconduct, or any negligence by the sponsor or his representative or the investigator.
c. Failure of IP to provide the intended therapeutic effect.
d. Adverse effects due to concomitant medication except standard care, used as part of the approved protocol.
e. For any harm to a fetus by the participation of a female in a clinical trial.
f. Any clinical trial procedures as per protocol.

Important documents to be reviewed in general:
- Protocol and protocol amendments
- Investigators Brochure
- Informed Consent form and Patient information sheet and its translation respective local language

- Clinical Trial Insurance Policy
- Clinical Trial Agreement
- An undertaking by the sponsor stating that the complete medical management is in accordance with rule 40 and an undertaking letter from the sponsor mentioning compensation in case of study related injury or death shall be provided in accordance with rule 39 of NDCT Rules 2019.
- Site Standard Operating Procedures

Review of Documents and preparation by sponsor, site, and EC:
All stakeholders involved in the SAE reporting process (including regulatory and project management teams of the sponsor/CRO, PI and study coordinator at the study site, and EC secretariat along with the Member Secretary) should be well-informed and trained on the SAE management and reporting guidelines released by the regulatory body.

The Sponsor shall have a list of documents at various stages of the process:
- Investigator Undertaking
- Aadhar Card
- Curriculum Vitae
- Medical Registration Certificate
- CT NOC
- CTRI Registration
- Protocol (version at the time of SAE) and protocol amendments
- Investigators Brochure (version at the time of SAE)
- Completed CRF
- CIOMS/ Sponsor Analysis
- Compensation if Paid

Investigator Should maintain and review the following documents in case of SAE:
- Copy of CT-NOC / CT permission letter (CDSCO)
- EC Registration Certificate [CDSCO]
- Completed Appendix XI [Table 5 on Sugam]
- Discharge summary [hospitalized patients]
- Death Certificate (if available)
- Autopsy report [if available]
- Lab investigation Reports (prior to and during clinical trials)

- Excel sheet of Lab investigations
- Signed ICF
- Protocol Ver. Copy
- Standard care of treatment/ Prescription
- CIOMS

Information of the Study Drug and Comparator
- Generic name of the drug
- Strength
- Units
- Route of administration
- Dosing frequency
- an indication of use
- Mechanism of action
- Brief Pharmacokinetic and Pharmacodynamic information
- Elimination T 1/2

Causality assessment in the case of SAE:
The assessment of the causal relationship of the event with the investigational product or trial related procedures should be done by the Ethics committee. Following points must be taken into consideration while performing causality assessment:
- Temporal sequence
- Previous experience/Drug information available
- Drug level in the system
- Alternative etiology
- Dechallenge / Rechallenge
- Plausibility
- Concomitant drugs
- Objective evidence
- Background epidemiological data

THE SEVENTH SCHEDULE of NDCT RULES 2019

FORMULAE TO DETERMINE THE QUANTUM OF COMPENSATION IN THE CASES OF CLINICAL TRIAL RELATED INJURY OR DEATH

The formula in case of clinical trial related death:

Compensation = (B x F x R) / 99.37
Where,

B = Base amount (i.e. 8 lacs)

F = Factor depending on the age of the trial subject as per Annexure 1 (based on the Workmen Compensation Act)

R = Risk Factor depending on the seriousness and severity of the disease, presence of co-morbidity and duration of disease of the trial subject at the time of enrolment in the clinical trial between a scale of 0.5 to 4 as under:

- 0.5 terminally ill patient (expected survival not more than (NMT) 6 months)
- 1.0 Patient with high risk (expected survival between 6 to 24 months)
- 2.0 Patient with moderate risk
- 3.0 Patient with mild risk
- 4.0 Healthy Volunteers or trial subject of no risk.

However, in case of patients whose expected mortality is 90% or more within 30 days, a fixed amount of Rs. 2 lacs should be given.[2]

2. Formula in case of clinical trial related injury (other than death):

For calculation of the quantum of compensation related to injury (other than death), the compensation shall be linked to the criteria considered for calculation of compensation in cases of death of the trial subject as referred to in section of this Schedule. The quantum of compensation in case of Clinical Trial related SAE should not exceed the quantum of compensation which would have been due for payment in Case of death of the trial subject since the loss of life is the maximum injury possible. As per the definition of SAE, the following sequelae other than death are possible in a clinical trial subject, in which the trial subject shall be entitled to compensation in case the SAE is related to the clinical trial.

(i) A permanent disability:
In case of SAE causing permanent disability to the trial subject, the quantum of compensation in case of 100% disability shall be 90% of the compensation which would have been due for payment to the nominee (s) in case of death of the trial subject.
The quantum for less than 100% disability will be proportional to the actual percentage of disability the trial subject has suffered.

Accordingly, the following formula shall be applicable for the determination of compensation:

Compensation = (C x D x 90) / (100 x 100)
Where:

D = Percentage disability the trial subject has suffered.
C = Quantum of Compensation which would have been due for payment to the trial subject's nominees) in case of death of the trial subject.

(ii) Congenital anomaly or birth defect:
The congenital anomaly or birth defect in a baby may occur due to participation of anyone or both the parent in clinical trial. Following situations may arise due to congenital anomaly or birth defect.
(a) Still birth;
(b) Early death due to anomaly;
(c) No death but deformity which can be fully corrected through appropriate intervention;
(d) Permanent disability (mental or physical).

The compensation in such cases would be a lump sum amount such that if that amount is kept by way of fixed deposit or alike, it shall bring a monthly interest amount which is approximately equivalent to half of minimum wage of the unskilled worker (in Delhi). The quantum of compensation in such cases of SAE shall be half of the base amount as per formula for determining the compensation for SAE resulting into death.

In case of birth defect leading to sub-clause (c) and (d) of this clause to any child, the medical management as long as required shall be provided by the Sponsor or his representative which will be over and above the financial compensation.

(iii) Chronic life-threatening disease; and
(iv) Reversible SAE in case it is resolved.
In the case of clinical trial-related SAE causing life-threatening disease and reversible SAE in case it is resolved, the quantum of the compensation would be linked to the number of days of hospitalisation of the trial subject. The compensation per day of hospitalization shall be equal to the wage loss. The wage loss per day shall be calculated based on the minimum wage of the unskilled worker (in Delhi).

Since, in case of hospitalisation of any patient not only does the patient loses his/her wage, there will be direct or indirect losses of various kind including inconvenience, wage loss of attendant, etc. The compensation per day of hospitalisation in such case shall be double the minimum wage.

Accordingly, following formula shall be applicable for determination of compensation:

Compensation = 2 X W X N.

Where,
W = Minimum wage per day of the unskilled worker (in Delhi)
N = Number of days of hospitalization
Factor (F) for calculating the amount of compensation

Age	Factor
Not more than...16	228.54
17	227.49
18	226.38
19	225.22
20	224.00
21	222.71
22	221.37
23	219.95
24	218.47
25	216.91
26	215.28
27	213.57
28	211.79
29	209.92
30	207.98
31	205.95
32	203.85
33	201.66
34	199.40
35	197.06
36	194.64
37	192.14
38	189.56
39	186.90
40	184.17
41	181.37
42	178.49
43	175.54
44	172.52
45	169.44
46	166.29
47	163.07

Age	Factor
41	181.37
42	178.49
43	175.54
44	172.52
45	169.44
46	166.29
47	163.07
48	159.80
49	156.47
50	153.09
51	149.67
52	146.20
53	142.68
54	139.13
55	135.56
56	131.95
57	128.33
58	124.70
59	121.05
60	117.41
61	113.77
62	110.14
63	106.52
64	102.93
65 or more	99.37

References:

1. International Conference on Harmonisation of Technical Requirements for Registration of Pharmaceuticals for Human Use. ICH Harmonised Tripartite Guideline for Good Clinical Practice E6. 1996. [Last accessed on 2020 Jul 23]. Available from: https://ichgcp.net/
2. New Drug and Clinical Trial Rule; 2019 Guideline. [Last accessed on 2020 Jul 23]. Available from: https://cdsco.gov.in/opencms/opencms/Pdf-documents/NewDrugs_CTRules_2019.pdf.
3. Nambiar I. Analysis of serious adverse event: Writing a narrative. Perspect Clin Res. 2018;9:103–6.
4. Sil A, Das NK. Ethics of safety reporting of a clinical trial. Indian J Dermatol. 2017;62:387–91. [PMC free article]
5. Drugs & Cosmetics Act; GSR 53E. 2013. [Last accessed on 2020 Jul 28]. Available from: https://cdsco.gov.in/opencms/opencms/en/Notifications/Gazette-Notifications/.
6. Choudhury K, Ghooi R. New rules for clinical trial-related injury and compensation. Indian J Med Ethics. 2013;10:197–200.

Chapter 17

Investigational product management

Mrs. Lakshmi Achuta, MRQA
MS Quality Management (BITS Pilani),
Master of Science (M.Sc.), Applied Botany,
Principal Strategic Advisor - Biotech,
Pharmaceuticals & Medical Devices, AshRin Bio,
Bengaluru, Karnataka

Abstract

Management of investigation product during the conduct of the clinical trial is very important and crucial aspect that comes under the scrutiny of regulatory agencies. It provides confidence that the entire activity was managed in a controlled manner. The investigational product(s) (including active comparator(s) and placebo, if applicable) is characterized as appropriate to the stage of development of the product(s), and is manufactured in accordance with any applicable GMP, and is coded and labelled in a manner that protects the blinding, if applicable. The labelling should comply with applicable regulatory requirement(s). Acceptable storage temperatures, storage conditions (e.g., protection from light), storage times, reconstitution fluids and procedures, and devices for product infusion, if any, should be determined. All involved parties (e.g., monitors, investigators, pharmacists, storage managers) should be aware of these requirements. Therefore this is an important topic. Investigational products related details are discussed in this article.

Objective: Understand the requirements and the relevance of Investigational product as per ICH GCP E6 (R2).

Management of investigation product during the conduct of the clinical trial is very important and crucial aspect that comes under the scrutiny of regulatory agencies. It provides confidence that the entire activity was managed in a controlled manner.

Principles of ICH GCP (2.12) state: *'Investigational products should be manufactured, handled, and stored in accordance with applicable good manufacturing practice (GMP). They should be used in accordance with the approved protocol.'*

The investigational product(s) (including active comparator(s) and placebo, if applicable) is characterized as appropriate to the stage of development of the product(s), and is manufactured in accordance with any applicable GMP, and is coded and labelled in a manner that protects the blinding, if applicable. The labelling should comply with applicable regulatory requirement(s). Acceptable storage temperatures, storage conditions (e.g., protection from light), storage times, reconstitution fluids and procedures, and devices for product infusion, if any, should be determined. All involved parties (e.g., monitors, investigators, pharmacists, storage managers) should be aware of these requirements. Investigational product(s) should be packaged to prevent contamination and unacceptable deterioration during transport and storage. In blinded trials, the coding system for the investigational product(s) should include a mechanism that permits rapid identification of the product(s) in case of a medical emergency

Corresponding author: Mrs. Lakshmi Achuta. Can be contacted at phone number+91 98803 03998
Email id: lakshmi.achuta@ashrinbio.com

but does not permit undetectable breaks of the blinding. If significant formulation changes are made in the investigational or comparator product(s) during clinical development, the results of any additional studies of the formulated product(s) (e.g., stability, dissolution rate, bioavailability) needed to assess whether these changes would significantly alter the pharmacokinetic profile of the product should be available prior to the use of the new formulation in clinical trials.

Investigational Product is supplied to the investigational site only after the Sponsor obtains all required documentation (e.g., approval / favourable opinion from IRB/IEC and regulatory authority(ies)). Written procedures include instructions that the investigator/institution should follow for the handling and storage of investigational product(s) for the trial and documentation thereof.

Investigational product accountability is very crucial during the conduct of the clinical trials. Procedures should be available to address adequate and safe receipt, handling, storage, dispensing, retrieval of unused product from subjects, and return of unused investigational product(s) to the sponsor (or alternative disposition if authorized by the sponsor and in compliance with the applicable regulatory requirement(s)). Sponsors ensure timely delivery of investigational product(s) to the investigator(s), maintain records that document shipment, receipt, disposition, return, and destruction of the investigational product(s); maintain a system for retrieving investigational products and documenting this retrieval (e.g., for deficient product recall, reclaim after trial completion, expired product reclaim), maintain a system for the disposition of unused investigational product(s) and for the documentation of this disposition.

Sponsors ensure that the investigational product should be stable over a period of use, maintain sufficient quantities of the investigational product(s) used in the trials to reconfirm specifications, should this become necessary, and maintain records of batch sample analyses and characteristics. To the extent stability permits, samples should be retained either until the analyses of the trial data are complete or as required by the applicable regulatory requirement(s), whichever represents the longer retention period.

Chain of custody is very critical during the conduct of the study. At the investigator site, the investigator assigns some or all of the investigator's/institution's duties for investigational product(s) accountability at the trial site(s) to a qualified pharmacist who is under the supervision of the investigator/institution, and should maintain records of the product's delivery to the trial site, the inventory at the site, the use by each subject, and the return to the sponsor or alternative disposition of unused product(s). These records should include dates, quantities, batch/serial numbers, expiration dates (if applicable), and the unique code numbers assigned to the investigational product(s) and trial subjects. Investigators should maintain records that document adequately that the subjects were provided the doses specified by the protocol and reconcile all investigational product(s) received from the sponsor.

The investigational product(s) should be stored as specified by the sponsor and in accordance with applicable regulatory requirement(s). The investigator should ensure that the investigational product(s) are used only in accordance with the approved protocol. The investigator, or a person designated by the investigator/institution, should explain the correct use of the investigational product(s) to each subject and should check, at intervals appropriate for the trial, that each subject is following the instructions properly.

During regulatory inspections, regulatory authorities / inspectors scrutinize the traceability of the investigational product from the regulatory approvals (if any, viz., import permission, etc.) to the receipt at the sponsor depot to shipment to the site, dispensing to the subject and usage. Documentation in terms of chain of custody should be available, allows tracking of product batch, review of shipping conditions, and accountability.

Investigational product(s) accountability at site through documentation indicates that the investigational product(s) have been used according to the protocol. It documents the final accounting of investigational product(s) received at the site, dispensed to subjects, returned by the subjects, and returned to sponsor. Documentation of investigational product destruction indicates destruction of unused investigational products by sponsor or at site (if destroyed at site).

Documentation related to investigational product management are essential documents which individually and collectively permit evaluation of the conduct of a trial and the quality of the data produced. These documents serve via reconstruction of activity to demonstrate the compliance of the investigator, sponsor and monitor with the standards of Good Clinical Practice and with all applicable regulatory requirements.

Conclusion:

Investigational products are manufactured, handled, and stored in accordance with applicable current good manufacturing practice (cGMP); and are used in accordance with the approved protocol.

Investigator Brochure provides appropriate use of the investigational product(s), as described in the protocol and in the product information provided by the Sponsor which enables the investigator to be thoroughly familiar with the investigational product (s).

Chain of custody ensures traceability of the Investigational Product from the relevant licenses / permits taken to the receipt, and storage as per the product requirements to subsequent shipment to Investigational site; distribution to the subjects. Subsequently, followed by destruction. All stakeholders should ensure that the accountability is documented.

References:

1. Integrated Addendum to ICH E6(R1): Guideline For Good Clinical Practice E6(R2) – 9th November, 2016
2. New Drugs and Clinical Trials Rules, 2019

Chapter 18

Current remote monitoring aspects in clinical trials quality & safety management systems using AI & ML tools: A Conceptual Framework

Mrs.Karishma Rampilla[1]. Dr.Giridhar kanuru[2], Charishma Jonnadula[3], Harsha.Alugula[4]

[1]Ms. Karishma Rampilla B.tech, M.tech, (Biotechnology), PGD clinical research, Director & Founder, Cavaxion Clinical Research Pvt Ltd., Hyderabad, Telangana.

[2]Dr.Giridhar kanuru, HOD biotechnology, KLUniversity

[3]Charishma Jonnadula, QA& Sr.CRC; Agarwal hospitals.

[4]Harsha.Alugula, CRC; Nakshtra hospitals

Abstract

To explore the current aspects of remote monitoring in clinical trials and its potential to enhance quality and safety management systems. Remote monitoring plays an important role in clinical trials by offering benefits that significantly impact the quality management of the studies. Through remote access to patient data and electronic health records, safety issues, adverse events, and protocol deviations can be promptly identified, enabling timely interventions, and safeguarding the well-being of trial participants. This aspect of remote monitoring is crucial in maintaining the highest standards of patient care throughout the trial. remote monitoring significantly improves efficiency in clinical trials. By eliminating the need for extensive travel and on-site visits, it reduces costs and saves valuable time. Monitors can remotely review source documents, electronic records, and study documentation, allowing them to focus on critical aspects of the trial. The proposed framework prototype consists of data collection module, data transmission module, and data analysis and prediction module. The data analytic and prediction module is the core section of the proposed framework tailored with data analysis. These datasets are pre-processed and transformed and then used to train and test the system, through different experimental analysis including bagging Support Vector Machine (SVM) and Artificial Neural Network (ANN). The outcome of the analysis presents classification into three different categories, such as fit, unfit, and undecided participants. These various classifications are used to determine if a participant should be allowed to continue in the trial or not.

Keywords: Clinical trial; Remote monitoring, QMS systems Framework; Monitoring; Physiological data; Wearable device.

Corresponding author: Mrs.Karishma Rampilla. Can be contacted at phone number+91 99082 30123.
Email id: Karishma.Rampilla@cavaxion.com

Introduction:

How it is applicable in day-to-day CT operations: Remote monitoring in clinical trials has become increasingly applicable in day-to-day operations, revolutionizing the way trials are conducted. By embracing this approach, researchers and stakeholders can overcome geographical barriers, streamline processes, and ensure seamless communication, ultimately leading to more efficient and successful trials. With remote monitoring, investigators can remotely access and review data, patient records, and study documentation, all in real-time [1]. This allows for immediate identification of potential issues or deviations from the protocol, enabling timely interventions and adjustments. Moreover, remote monitoring facilitates proactive management of patient safety by enabling continuous surveillance of adverse events and ensuring prompt reporting and appropriate actions[2]. Additionally, the convenience of remote monitoring reduces travel requirements and related costs, allowing monitors to allocate more time and resources to critical aspects of the trial. This dynamic approach not only enhances the quality and safety management systems but also accelerates the pace of clinical research, contributing to the advancement of medical knowledge and improved patient care.

The emergence of technology has introduced wearable devices in healthcare. Internet of Things (IoT) is a system that integrates physical objects, software, and hardware to communicate with each other. Population increase, limited healthcare resources, and increase in medical costs has made IoT-based technologies necessary to solve challenges in healthcare[3]. IoT has several applications in healthcare, ranging from remote monitoring to smart sensors and medical device integration. Internet-of-things has made healthcare smart by integrating smart wearable medical devices used to monitor patient health status in real time. These wearables devices are capable of overseeing health and wellness of a patient and sending biofeedback to a hub in real time.

Mobile health can be said to be the application of mobile monitoring devices in medical and public healthcare[4]

What Guidelines says?

The guidelines regarding remote monitoring in clinical trials emphasize its importance in ensuring the quality and safety of study conduct. These guidelines provide valuable recommendations and best practices to help researchers and sponsors effectively implement remote monitoring strategies while maintaining compliance with regulatory requirements. The guidelines suggest that remote monitoring should be supported by appropriate technology and secure systems for data transfer and storage[5]. The chosen platforms should meet the necessary standards for data protection and confidentiality, ensuring that patient information remains secure throughout the monitoring process. The guidelines emphasize the importance of training and support for all stakeholders involved in remote monitoring. Investigators, site staff, and monitors should receive adequate training on the use of remote monitoring tools and systems. This ensures their proficiency in utilizing the technology effectively and aligning with the established protocols and procedures. The guidelines highlight the need for clear communication channels between monitors, investigators, and site staff. Regular virtual meetings and check-ins are encouraged to facilitate collaboration, address questions, and provide ongoing support. Having well-defined procedures in place helps maintain consistency and adherence to regulatory guidelines[6].

what are the common problems seen in day-to-day implementation?

Technological Challenges: One common problem encountered is technological issues. Remote monitoring relies heavily on technology infrastructure, including internet connectivity, software platforms, and data transfer systems. Technical glitches, connectivity disruptions, or compatibility issues between different systems can hinder the seamless implementation of remote monitoring.

Data Security Concerns: Data security is a significant concern in remote monitoring. Protecting patient confidentiality and ensuring data integrity are paramount. Issues such as unauthorized access, data breaches, or inadequate encryption measures can compromise the security of sensitive patient information[7]. Implementing robust data security protocols and complying with relevant regulations are crucial in mitigating these risks.

Training and Proficiency: Another challenge is ensuring that all stakeholders involved in remote monitoring are adequately trained and proficient in using the technology. Investigators, site staff, and monitors need to be familiar with remote monitoring tools and systems to maximize their effectiveness. Insufficient training can lead to difficulties in navigating the platforms, understanding the monitoring process, or properly interpreting and reporting data. [8]

Regulatory Compliance: Meeting regulatory requirements can be a complex aspect of remote monitoring. Ensuring adherence to Good Clinical Practice (GCP) guidelines, local regulatory guidelines, and data privacy laws is essential. Failure to comply with these regulations can lead to serious consequences, including data rejection or even trial suspension. Staying updated with evolving regulations and maintaining meticulous documentation are vital for maintaining compliance.

Related works:

How such problems can be removed. What cautions can help?

To address the common problems encountered in the day-to-day implementation of remote monitoring in clinical trials, several precautions can be taken[9]. By being proactive and implementing the following measures, stakeholders can overcome challenges and ensure a smooth and successful remote monitoring process:

Robust Technological Infrastructure: Ensuring a reliable and secure technological infrastructure is essential.

This includes having stable internet connectivity, utilizing reputable software platforms, and regularly updating systems to avoid compatibility issues. Regular maintenance and testing of technology can help identify and resolve any potential glitches before they impact the monitoring process.

Data Security Measures: Implementing stringent data security measures is crucial to safeguard patient information. This involves utilizing encryption techniques, access controls, and secure data transfer protocols. Regular assessments of data security practices and compliance with relevant regulations can help mitigate risks and maintain the confidentiality and integrity of data.

Comprehensive Training and Proficiency: Providing thorough training to all stakeholders involved in remote monitoring is key. Investigators, site staff, and monitors should receive comprehensive training on using remote monitoring tools, understanding the monitoring process, and interpreting data accurately[10]. Regular refresher training sessions can help reinforce knowledge and address any proficiency gaps.

Adherence to Regulatory Guidelines: Strict adherence to regulatory guidelines, such as GCP and local regulations, is critical for successful remote monitoring. Staying updated with the latest regulatory requirements and conducting regular internal audits can help identify and rectify any compliance gaps. Maintaining meticulous documentation and record-keeping practices ensures transparency and facilitates regulatory inspections and audits[11]. The system was used to collect physiological signs from patients using a wearable sensor, the collected data is transmitted to the hospital server where the doctors and nurses can access for analysis, hence used to determine the health status of the patient. Knowledge of the medical personals such as the medical doctors and nurses are transferred into the system, such as standard body physiological parameters and symptoms of some chronic diseases such as diabetics, high blood pressure, asthma etc. is used to monitor the patient, to determine the health status of the patient using ensemble classifier.

Interpretation of international guidelines in comparison with Indian guidelines if applicable

International guidelines, such as the International Council for Harmonisation of Technical Requirements for Pharmaceuticals for Human Use (ICH), is an initiative that brings together the regulatory bodies pharmaceutical sectors for clinical trial conduct [12]. These guidelines focus on ensuring data integrity, patient safety, and adherence to Good Clinical Practice (GCP) principles. Indian guidelines, issued by regulatory bodies like the Central Drugs Standard Control Organization (CDSCO), are specific to the Indian factors. They may align with international guidelines to a large extent but can also have certain country-specific considerations. These guidelines outline regulatory requirements, ethical considerations, and procedures for clinical trials conducted in India. When interpreting international and Indian guidelines, it is essential to consider any variations in local regulatory requirements, such as specific documentation or reporting obligations, as per Indian regulations[13].

Recent challenge due to technology advancement or change in recent guidelines.

In recent times, the rapid advancement of technology and the release of updated guidelines have presented new challenges and considerations in the implementation of remote monitoring in clinical trials. While these developments bring significant benefits, they also require careful attention and adaptation[14]. With the increasing use of digital platforms and remote monitoring tools, ensuring robust data privacy and security has become a paramount concern. The introduction of new technologies, such as wearables, mobile health applications, and electronic patient-reported outcome tools, has expanded the possibilities of remote monitoring. However, integrating these technologies seamlessly into existing systems and ensuring their compatibility with regulatory requirements can pose challenges. Obtaining informed consent remotely has gained prominence in the context of remote monitoring[15].

Recent guidelines provide insights into the ethical considerations and regulatory requirements surrounding remote informed consent procedures. These guidelines outline the need for clear communication, adequate information provision, and mechanisms to verify participant understanding and willingness to participate, all while maintaining the ethical principles of autonomy and voluntariness. As technology advances and global collaborations in clinical research grow, there is a greater need for regulatory harmonization. Recent guidelines may aim to align regulatory approaches across regions to facilitate the acceptance and recognition of remote monitoring practices. Harmonized guidelines can streamline processes, reduce duplication of efforts, and promote consistency in the implementation of remote monitoring in clinical trials.

How to adopt to such change?

Adopting to changes brought about by technology advancements and evolving guidelines in the field of remote monitoring requires a proactive and adaptable approach[16]. Regularly stay informed about the latest technology advancements, regulatory guidelines, and best practices in remote monitoring. Keep track of industry publications, attend conferences, and engage in professional networks to stay up to date with the latest trends and developments. Conduct a thorough assessment of your current remote monitoring processes, systems, and infrastructure. Identify any gaps or areas that need improvement to align with the changing landscape. This evaluation will help you understand the specific changes required and provide a foundation for strategic decision-making. Provide comprehensive training and education to all stakeholders involved in remote monitoring, including investigators, site staff, and monitors. Ensure they are well-versed in the latest technologies, regulatory requirements, and best practices. This will empower them to adapt to the changes effectively and confidently utilize remote monitoring tools and systems[17]. Stay vigilant about regulatory updates and requirements pertaining to remote monitoring. Maintain a proactive approach in adapting to regulatory changes and ensure ongoing compliance. Collaborate with regulatory bodies, seek their guidance, and implement necessary measures to meet regulatory expectations.

Additional information to improve quality and audit outcomes in remote monitoring

Adopt a risk-based approach to monitoring, focusing resources on high-risk areas and critical data points. RBM allows for targeted monitoring activities, ensuring efficient use of resources while maintaining data quality and patient safety. Create detailed data management plans that outline data handling procedures, data quality checks, and data reconciliation processes. Clearly define roles and responsibilities for data management tasks, ensuring consistency and accuracy throughout the trial. Establish standardized processes and documentation templates for remote monitoring activities[18]. This promotes consistency, reduces variability, and improves efficiency in data review and documentation. Leverage centralized data monitoring tools that provide real-time access to trial data, allowing for efficient data review and analysis. These tools often include built-in data visualizations, query management systems, and customizable reporting features, streamlining the monitoring process and facilitating timely identification of data discrepancies. Regularly perform internal audits and quality assurance checks to evaluate the effectiveness of remote monitoring practices. These audits can help identify any gaps or areas for improvement, enabling proactive measures to be taken. Address any findings promptly and implement corrective actions to enhance data quality and compliance. Prepare for external audits and inspections by regulatory authorities or sponsors[19]. Maintain meticulous documentation, ensure adherence to regulatory requirements, and implement robust quality control measures.

Proactively address any findings from audits or inspections and take appropriate actions to improve overall quality and compliance. Stay informed about regulatory updates and changes related to remote monitoring. Regularly review guidance documents, attend regulatory webinars or workshops, and actively participate in industry discussions. Ensuring compliance with the latest regulatory requirements is crucial to maintaining quality and achieving favourable audit outcomes.

Limitations:

Remote monitoring, lacks the direct physical interaction between monitors and site staff that traditional on-site monitoring provides. This can hinder the ability to observe certain non-verbal cues or engage in face-to-face discussions, potentially impacting the depth of understanding and relationship-building between monitors and site personnel. Remote monitoring relies heavily on technology, making it susceptible to technical challenges[20]. Connectivity issues, software malfunctions, or compatibility problems between different systems can disrupt the smooth operation of remote monitoring. Adequate technical support and contingency plans are essential to minimize the impact of these challenges. It relies on electronic data capture systems and remote access to study documentation. Some site visits or physical document reviews may still be necessary to address these limitations. Monitors may have limited visibility into the site environment, such as the physical layout, site-specific processes, or potential distractions during data collection. This limitation requires a high level of trust and collaboration between monitors and site staff to ensure data integrity. It is essential to ensure compliance with regulatory guidelines. Different regulatory authorities may have specific requirements regarding remote monitoring practices, data security, and documentation. Staying updated with evolving regulations and adapting remote monitoring strategies accordingly is crucial. Language barriers or differences in communication styles may affect the effectiveness of remote monitoring, requiring additional measures such as translation services or cultural sensitivity training to ensure clear and accurate communication [21].

Results: AI and ML continue to be used in diverse ways in clinical trials Here are a few keyways machine learning can change how you develop trials and test their feasibility, helping drug manufacturing organization save time and money. Benefits attained in this type of e-clinical trials Review of Safety /efficacy/marketing of drug, Number of drug and mode of action is same CT helps to rule out this, identify other trials that might have valuable data for cross sharing and integration. AI technology in clinical trials has the potential to speed up cohort selection and pin clinical trial. Cavaxion Mobile application will add Data collection, Data merging, Patient selection, Immediate safety reporting to sponsor, IRB, EC, Virtual PI meeting, AI data analysis, Monitoring. Virtual De centralized clinical trials, Virtual patient safety reporting, Laboratory data merging capacity. This AI mobile application developed will help give 100 X faster Data, Patient leads, Monitoring, safety reporting, site management, medical coding. All in one clinical trial. Mobile platform act,ict SUBJECT RECRUITMENT & TRIAL FINDING Patient reported Outcomes, Subject Monitoring, Electronic Data Capture & Clinical Trial Management Systems, Imaging & Scan disease detection technology.

Conclusion: In conclusion, remote monitoring in clinical trials offers immense potential for enhancing the quality and safety management systems. While certain challenges may arise during its implementation, such as technological issues, data security concerns, training requirements, communication hurdles, regulatory compliance, and resistance to change, these can be overcome with the right strategies and support. By addressing these common problems proactively, researchers and stakeholders can fully harness the benefits of remote monitoring[22]. It allows for efficient data collection, improved patient safety, streamlined processes, real-time oversight, and cost savings. we can successfully navigate the challenges and embrace the transformative power of remote monitoring, ultimately leading to more effective and successful clinical trials.

Reference :

1. Muurling, Marijn, et al. "Ethical challenges of using remote monitoring technologies for clinical research: A case study of the role of local research ethics committees in the RADAR-AD study." Plos one 18.7 (2023): e028580

2. Boric-Lubecke, Olga, et al. "E-healthcare: Remote monitoring, privacy, and security." 2014 IEEE MTT-S international microwave symposium (IMS2014). IEEE, 2014

3. Crossley, George H., et al. "The CONNECT (Clinical Evaluation of Remote Notification to Reduce Time to Clinical Decision) trial: the value of wireless remote monitoring with automatic clinician alerts." Journal of the American College of Cardiology 57.10 (2011): 1181-1189

4. Liao, Yue, et al. "The future of wearable technologies and remote monitoring in health care." American Society of Clinical Oncology Educational Book 39 (2019): 115-121.

5. Noah, Benjamin, et al. "Impact of remote patient monitoring on clinical outcomes: an updated meta-analysis of randomized controlled trials." NPJ digital medicine 1.1 (2018): 20172.

6. Apostolaros, Maria, et al. "Legal, regulatory, and practical issues to consider when adopting decentralized clinical trials: recommendations from the clinical trials transformation initiative." Therapeutic innovation & regulatory science 54 (2020): 779-787

7. Hirsch, Irl B., et al. "Incorporating site-less clinical trials into drug development: a framework for action." Clinical therapeutics 39.5 (2017): 1064-1076.

8. Hashem, Hasan, et al. "Obstacles and considerations related to clinical trial research during the COVID-19 pandemic." Frontiers in medicine 7 (2020): 598038

9. Agrafiotis, Dimitris K., et al. "Risk-based monitoring of clinical trials: an integrative approach." Clinical therapeutics 40.7 (2018): 1204-1212

10. Houston, Lauren, et al. "Clinical researchers' lived experiences with data quality monitoring in clinical trials: a qualitative study." BMC Medical Research Methodology 21 (2021): 1-15.

11. Izmailova, Elena S., Robert Ellis, and Christopher Benko. "Remote monitoring in clinical trials during the COVID☐19 pandemic." Clinical and Translational Science 13.5 (2020): 838-841.

12. Farias, Frederico Arriaga Criscuoli de, et al. "Remote patient monitoring: a systematic review." Telemedicine and e-Health 26.5 (2020): 576-583.

13. Yamada, Osamu, et al. "Clinical trial monitoring effectiveness: remote risk-based monitoring versus on-site monitoring with 100% source data verification." Clinical trials 18.2 (2021): 158-167.

14. Love, Sharon B., et al. "What is the purpose of clinical trial monitoring?." Trials 23.1 (2022): 836

15. Esposito, Pasquale, and Antonio Dal Canton. "Clinical audit, a valuable tool to improve quality of care: General methodology and applications in nephrology." *World journal of nephrology* 3.4 (2014): 249.

16. Hut-Mossel, Lisanne, et al. "Understanding how and why audits work in improving the quality of hospital care: a systematic realist review." *PloS one* 16.3 (2021): e0248677.

17. Varma, Niraj, and Renato Pietro Ricci. "Impact of remote monitoring on clinical outcomes." *Journal of cardiovascular electrophysiology* 26.12 (2015): 1388-1395.

18. Royle, Jennifer K., et al. "Technology clinical trials: Turning innovation into patient benefit." *Digital Health* 7 (2021): 20552076211012131.

19. Geoghegan, Cindy, et al. "Learning from patient and site perspectives to develop better digital health trials: recommendations from the Clinical Trials Transformation Initiative." *Contemporary Clinical Trials Communications* 19 (2020): 100636.

20. Rosa, Carmen, et al. "Using digital technologies in clinical trials: Current and future applications." *Contemporary clinical trials* 100 (2021): 106219.

21. Rudd, Brittany N., Molly Davis, and Rinad S. Beidas. "Integrating implementation science in clinical research to maximize public health impact: a call for the reporting and alignment of implementation strategy use with implementation outcomes in clinical research." *Implementation Science* 15.1 (2020): 1-11.

22. Biggs, Katie, et al. "Challenges in the design, planning and implementation of trials evaluating group interventions." *Trials* 21.1 (2020): 1-16.

23. Stensland, Kristian D., et al. "Applying implementation frameworks to the clinical trial context." *Implementation Science Communications* 3.1 (2022): 1-13.

24. Saxena, Pikee, and Rohit Saxena. "Clinical trials: changing regulations in India." Indian journal of community medicine: official publication of Indian Association of Preventive & Social Medicine 39.4 (2014): 197

25. Kamnoore, Kalpana, et al. "Regulatory requirements for conducting clinical trials in India." Research Journal of Pharmacy and Technology 13.3 (2020): 1517-1522.

26. Das, Nilay Kanti, and Amrita Sil. "Evolution of ethics in clinical research and ethics committee." Indian journal of dermatology 62.4 (2017): 373.

27. Bhave, Amita, and Suresh Menon. "Regulatory environment for clinical research: Recent past and expected future." Perspectives in clinical research 8.1 (2017): 11.

28. George, Bobby, Shrinivas Krishnarao Kulkarni, and Nilima A. Kshirsagar. "Regulatory Requirements and Quality Standards in India's Clinical Trials Journey." Drug Discovery and Drug Development: The Indian Narrative (2021): 283-302

Chapter 19

Misconduct and Fraud in Clinical research and its consequences

Mr. Manish Singh Yadav, MS (Analytical Instrumentation and Chemical analysis),
(PhD Bio-analytical Chemistry Pursuing),
Founder and CEO of Ethixinn CRS,
Madhya Pradesh

Abstract

With the advancement of scientific practices through continuous learning, clinical research has progressed significantly in the past two decades. At the same time, technological advancements and new regulatory requirements have propelled local and international regulatory agencies to bring about constructive improvements to their regulatory guidance and other relevant documents *(ICH M10-BMV, ICH E6(R3), and OECD, MHRA, and WHO-Data Integrity Guidelines)*. Thus, the dynamism of Clinical research demands not only sound Scientific Knowledge but also an excellent understanding of Quality and Regulatory requirements, and Ethics is the focal point in all aspects.

Some of the management and researchers may not be able to cope with techno-commercial pressures while achieving their routine conduct and research targets in exceedingly sophisticated and highly demanding research settings like CROs and R&D centres, and subsequently may be distracted from the ethics and the basic moral values resulting in misconduct and even fraud, thus compromising the rights, safety, and well being of trial subjects and so the credibility of clinical trial data.

Compliance with GCP standards and fraud prevention strategies ensure the proper and ethical conduct of trials while preventing, or at least reducing, the chances of misconduct and fraud. This is why it is crucial for all research professionals to understand and be familiar with GCP and allied good practices (GxP). Compliance with the global standard provides public assurance that the rights, safety, and well-being of trial subjects are protected, as are the trial data. Only by maintaining such systems, policies, and practices can fraud and misconduct in clinical research be minimised. We believe that a thorough understanding of clinical research dynamism, highly demanding research settings, and characteristics of fraud and misconduct can direct the researcher to devise a workable fraud-prevention strategy, which is a need of the hour.

Key words: *Clinical Research dynamism, GCP, Frauds, Misconduct, fraud prevention strategy*

Corresponding author: Mr. Manish Singh Yadav. Can be contacted at phone number+91 9979856040.
Email id: manish.yadav@ethixinn.com

Introduction:

Clinical research science has progressed significantly in the past two decades, and the advancement and learning that come from progressive and purposeful innovations are invaluable. Such levels of transformation signify the highly dynamic nature of clinical research. To cope with its ever-increasing demand, it is imperative to follow correct scientific practices, have adequate knowledge of the principal and allied sciences, and have technological innovations backed up by the incessant efforts of clinical researchers and medical practitioners.

The conceptualization, creation, and implementation of an appropriate 'Quality Management System (QMS)' for a bioanalytical lab and CRO necessitate focused and sustained efforts from the doers (analysts, laboratory professionals), quality professionals (QC/QM/QA), as well as the management (leadership). With inference from decades of globalised practices and hands-on experience, it is clearly understood that quality is a culture-driven phenomenon that needs to be inculcated in professionals and incorporated into the working culture of an organisation at the very onset.

Clinical research makes a significant contribution to medical practice, and it is therefore expected that all clinical research be conducted in accordance with the highest standards of research practice. Therefore, it is expected that the research staff fully comply with local regulations and guidelines and with the principles of the ICH-GCP Guideline. Misconduct can occur at any stage of the research process and often results when researchers seek to avoid negative consequences, gain prestige, or receive further funding based on their data.

Understanding Fraud and Misconduct:

By definition, **Fraud** is an intentional deception made for personal gain or to damage another individual, for instance, by intentionally falsifying and/or fabricating the trial or research data and misleadingly reporting the results. **Misconduct** may not be an intentional action or behaviour but rather an act of poor management that falls short of good ethical, quality, and scientific standards, but the effects may be very much the same as those caused by fraud. Research misconduct is the end of a person's research career and, in many cases, results in job termination.

Fraud includes both acts of *omission (*consciously not divulging the data) and *commission (*consciously altering or fabricating the data). In other words, Fraud doesn't include honest error, but deliberate and repeated non-compliance with GCP (*subject safety, study protocol, study-specific conditions*) can be considered fraud. Fraud can be encountered anywhere, including in processing, Designing, Performing, recording, supervising, reviewing, or reporting research results.

Anyone or all stakeholders or whoever involved in clinical research operations, like Sponsors, hospitals, sites, and CROs, Investigators, Co-investigators, Study coordinators, nurses, Data Management Personnel, Lab personnel, IEC and IRB staff, Clinical Research associates, and also FDA and Regulatory agencies (as only 3% of FDA inspections uncover serious GCP violations resulting in warning letters), are prone to commit frauds, intentionally or unintentionally, and hence get blamed for misconduct and fraud.

Government agencies treat fraud and research misconduct very seriously, as research misconduct can be the end of a person's research career. Many cases result in job termination. Considering the severity and impact of non-compliance, misconduct, and fraud, such sequential and subsequent fraudulent actions can severely impact not only the Business (Prosecution, Product Recall, Closing), Industry (Loss of Reputation, Business), Company (Loss of Reputation, Sales, share values), Employee (Loss of Jobs, Civil money penalties), but also the Country (Loss of Reputation, Industry, Public Health).

Causes of Fraud and Misconduct:

Working in an exceedingly sophisticated clinical research environment demands laser-sharp focus and tireless efforts of clinical researchers and all stakeholders; a slight noncompliance may lead to serious non-performance. It is normal to have errors in trials, and most are unintentional as they are usually caused by misunderstanding or inattention to detail. The impacts of unintentional or minor errors on study results are not as significant since they are traceable and easily corrected once they are caught. Errors can be eliminated, or at least reduced, through various means of Auditing, Monitoring, Reviewing, and Trending (trend analysis of study or statistical data).

When the question of causes of fraud and misconduct is asked of clinical researchers, prominent causes strike the mind. When it comes to analysing the causes of fraud and misconduct in the current research and regulatory scenario, certain prominent causes (but not limited to) strike the mind as too much reliance on human practices, insufficient

Education and understanding (WHY), lack of resources (staff, time, subjects, budgets), lack of training (GCP/GLP/GDP/Hands On), lack of regulatory oversight, laziness (instant Success, lack of knowledge, and greed), and loss of interest.

Further, relevant causes can be encountered as pressure to perform (projects, timelines, appraisals), fear of mistakes, loss of reputation, loss of performance appraisal, fearful-depressed-defensive staff, high staff turnover, unusually fast recruitment, or company or organisational culture. It is believed that company culture flows from top to bottom, further deeming that the systems, processes, and procedures (SOPs) can be fixed and improved but not the people, like behavioural change or creating a quality culture.

Data Identifier for Fraud and Misconduct:

In routine research conduct and reporting, certain implausible trends or patterns can be helpful to identify frauds, such as 100% drug compliance, identical lab or ECG results, no SAEs reported, subjects adhering preferably to a visit schedule or protocol conditions, perfect efficacy responses for all subjects, questionable subject visit dates (Sundays, holidays, or staff vacations), subject visits that cannot be verified in the medical chart or appointment schedule, and data that contains "digit preference—some digits used more frequently than others (0, 5, even digits).

Other implausible trends or patterns can be considered as submission of 'too perfect' data, dismissive or vague responses' to direct questioning, patterns or 'trends emerging from case report forms', e.g., bracketing, empty forms, striking off, trying to hide something, use of a single pen or handwriting style, etc., review date entries—are they logical?—examination of IMP supplies, examination of source data, site data not consistent with other centres (statistical outlier), fast recruitment, and source records lack an audit trail—no signatures and dates of persons completing documentation.

Fraud Detection Strategy (FDS):

In some instances, the deviations appear to go beyond innocent error and may constitute fraud, misconduct, or gross negligence. Fraud would soon be discovered if large amounts of data appeared after only a brief period of time, since other researchers in the group are fully aware that data collection can take several years. Many research institutions also have their own bodies and routines for monitoring the ethical and quality aspects of ongoing research projects.

A few strategies to detect frauds are to begin with expecting the fraud, just start from the assumption that records are 'bogus', ask questions like missing, altered, or inconsistent data, offer to retrieve records by yourself, keep pulling on loose ends, challenge the investigator to explain the suspicious data, be suspicious of blame shifting, remind the investigator that he or she is responsible for study conduct, and cultivate *whistleblowers* (pay attention to staff complaints, establish rapport, and be approachable). Many fraud cases are uncovered by *staff whistleblowers, who* are an integral part of the fraud detection process and may have an ethical commitment to reporting fraud at the organisational and/or global level.

Fraud Prevention Strategy– Mindset:

A specific plan for fraud prevention indicates a strong focus on *the mindset* of clinical and quality staff. A quality auditor or monitor, when reviewing the validation or study packages, has to imbibe the mindset of an FDA inspector who thinks, behaves, acts, and asks questions like the FDA. He is supposed to ask questions like "Does it look right" and/or "Do the conduct and data support the overall package". Further, management should come up with specific plans for inculcating the mindset of proper conduct and data handling along with core quality messages where everything is important, everyone is responsible, and nothing is too small or too big, keeping the "Organisational Quality Culture" as a top priority amongst all as "Culture always flows from top to bottom".

Fraud prevention strategy– Actions:

At the management level, all attempts are made to eliminate all types of occurrences. Training and education are key to preventing serious misconduct and fraud. It is Management's responsibility to ensure that all who are involved in research understand the conditions and principles of GCP and the individual responsibilities pertaining to them. Going ahead, robust procedures should be adopted to recruit reliable and capable research staff and obtain appropriate evidence of past education, qualifications, experience, and references.

A fraud prevention strategy should be devised at the organisational level through written and approved detailed policies, SOPs, or procedures. Among them all, devising an efficient Quality Management System (QMS) is the most important fraud prevention strategy. QMS should be conceptualised, developed, implemented, and run based on 'sound science' and practicality that is consistent, accurate, practical, flexible (to cope with the dynamic nature of clinical research), and eventually fit for purpose' and able to produce a consistent and accurate outcome.

Fraud protection from the QMS and QA front can be initiated by auditing your own processes through "Meta-analysis," which includes initiating the gap assessment or audit of nonconformance, periodic audit of long-term paper data archives and electronic data, appropriate closeout gap assessment along with full-flagged CAPA, strengthening the Internal quality audits to established research conduct and integrity controls to ensure continuous compliance, and regular review of audit trails. Further, *Meta-analysis* of multiple methods or projects using trending (finding patterns) and the latest audit principles

As a fraud prevention strategy during pre-study evaluation, the sponsor should carefully scrutinise the following: sites for interest in the study, stability of the staff, investigator and staff interactions, work load, and Training like GCP training for Everyone involved in the clinical trial operations or process. CRAs should be experts on the protocol, particularly the parameters that determine eligibility (inclusion and exclusion criteria) and primary efficacy end-points. The sponsor should further emphasise their policy on fraud at the initiation visit. Institutions should setup systems to encourage "fraud reporting" and protect whistleblowers.

A generic plan of fraud prevention starts with good quality standards and industry practices like imbibing appropriate analytical security controls, good documentation, and data management along with anticipation of any scope for automation plans or actions, protecting the data and ensuring it is being kept in 'proper' locations, periodic review of computer systems, acquired data, and SOPs to ensure data quality, training the employees on proper data as everyone is responsible for good development practice, and periodic training and awareness sessions on SOPs and current GCP/GDP Guidelines.

Conclusion:

It is believed that "every problem comes with its own inherent solution". First of all, *Fraud and Misconduct* should be understood to the core with respect to the dynamism and scientific, quality, and regulatory requirements of clinical research. A thorough understanding of the causes, identifiers, detection strategies, and prevention strategies of fraud and misconduct is deemed necessary to devise remedial actions. Addressing research fraud and fraudulence requires an inclusive focus on informing researchers and clinical staff on reporting and dealing with unethical practices.

There should be a greater focus on quality rather than Quantity. In continuation, an effective way to survive in clinical research is to update your tools— knowledge and resources—with the time to meet the current scientific-quality-regulatory standards and to adopt inspection-ready and inspector-friendly practices. Besides, sound scientific practices and research ethics should contribute to the promotion of sound clinical research and help prevent misconduct and fraud in clinical research.

References:

1. Journal of Pre-Clinical and Clinical Research, 2010, Vol 4, No 2, 158-160. Review. www.jpccr.eu

2. Coping up with dynamism of Data Integrity & management in Regulated Bioanalysis for BA/BE studies. Dr. Manish Yadav – CEO & Founder, Ethixinn

Chapter 20

Clinical trial's role in therapeutics and building guidelines for treatment of patients

Dr. Sanjeev Gupta[1] and Dr Ravindra Kumar[2]

[1]Dr. Sanjeev Gupta MBBS (MD Moscow), MD Pharmacology, Associate Professor, Dept of Pharmacology, Govt Medical College, Kathua, J & K.

[2]Dr Ravindra Kumar G MBBS, MD Pharamcology Assistant Prof, Dept of Pharmacology SVMC- Tirupati

Abstract

Clinical trials play a crucial role in advancing therapeutics and establishing evidence-based guidelines for treatment. These trials are the primary way that researchers determine if a new form of treatment or prevention, such as a new drug or medical device, is safe and effective in humans. The most important step in clinical trials is to study the safety and efficacy of a new medicine in human subjects. Other aims of clinical research include testing ways to diagnose a disease early, sometimes before there are symptoms. Clinical trials also help in finding approaches to prevent a health problem, including in people who are healthy but at increased risk of developing a disease, and improving the quality of life for people living with a life-threatening disease or chronic health problem. In this article, an attempt has been made to describe the role of clinical trials in building therapeutic guidelines for various diseases.

Introduction

Clinical trials play a crucial role in advancing therapeutics and establishing evidence-based guidelines for treatment. These trials are the primary way that researchers determine if a new form of treatment or prevention, such as a new drug, or medical device, is safe and effective in humans.

In all 4 phases of clinical trials, even though phases 1, 2, and 3 are focused on safety and efficacy, phase 3 gathers additional information from several hundred to a few thousand people by studying different populations and different dosages and comparing the intervention with other drugs or treatment approaches. After phase 3, the phase 4 trial takes place when approval from the FDA is received. Here, the treatment's effectiveness and safety are monitored in large, diverse populations. Sometimes, side effects may not become clear until more people have used the drug or device over a longer period of time. Because of that, clinical trials are designed in such a way to minimise harmful side effects while simultaneously increasing the effectiveness of new treatment options. And the most important step carried out by clinical trials is to study the safety and efficacy of a new medicine in human subjects.

Corresponding author: Dr. Sanjeev Gupta. Can be contacted at phone number+91 94197 63076
Email id: drsanjeevmow@gmail.com

Other aims of clinical research include:

- Testing ways to diagnose a disease early, sometimes before there are symptoms.

- Finding approaches to prevent a health problem, including in people who are healthy but at increased risk of developing a disease.

- Improving the quality of life for people living with a life-threatening disease or chronic health problem.

Patients' participation in clinical research:

- Help researchers learn about health, illness, or treatments.

- Be a part of discovering health information that may help others in the future.

- Possibly get a drug or medical device that is not yet approved to be used by people with a certain health condition.

Here are some ways in which clinical trials contribute to therapeutic and guideline development:

Assessing Treatment Safety: Clinical trials carefully monitor participants for adverse effects of the tested treatment. This helps identify potential safety concerns and ensure that treatments are not causing harm to patients by allowing researchers and regulatory authorities to establish guidelines for managing and minimising potential risks.

Evaluating Treatment Efficacy: Clinical trials are structured to measure the effectiveness of a treatment in achieving the desired outcomes. This helps determine if a new therapy is better than existing treatments or if it offers additional benefits.

It also allows testing and monitoring the effect of a medication or treatment on a large population to ensure that the improvement as a result of any medication or treatment is not for only one person but for a large number of people.

Comparing Treatments: In comparative clinical trials, compare the new treatment under investigation with existing standard treatments or a placebo (an inactive substance). These comparative studies help determine if the new therapy is superior, equivalent, or inferior to existing options. The results contribute to the selection of the most effective treatment options, leading to improved guidelines for clinical practice.

Clinical trials improve healthcare services by raising the standards of treatment.

Optimising Dosages and Regimens: Clinical trials help determine the optimal dosages and treatment schedules by balancing between maximum effectiveness and acceptable side effects. These findings are essential for developing treatment guidelines for different patient populations. New treatment approaches may help people live longer and with less pain or disability.

Identifying Target Populations: Clinical trials help identify which patient populations are most likely to benefit from a specific treatment. This allows medical professionals to tailor therapies to individual patients, increasing the likelihood of successful outcomes.

Tailoring treatments to specific populations: Clinical trials often include diverse groups of participants, including different age groups, genders, ethnicities, and individuals with specific medical conditions. This approach helps identify any variations in treatment response across populations. The resulting data guides the development of personalised treatment guidelines, taking individual characteristics into account and optimising therapeutic outcomes.

Generating Evidence-Based Data: The results of well-designed clinical trials provide valuable data that serves as the foundation for evidence-based medicine. This data is essential for making informed decisions about treatment guidelines and standards of care.

As clinical trials are conducted as per structured guidelines, data can be useful to healthcare professionals in delivering consistent, effective, and standardised care to patients.

Long-Term Safety and Efficacy: Some clinical trials continue to follow participants over an extended period, even after the treatment is approved and on the market. This provides data on the long-term safety and efficacy of the treatment, which is essential for ongoing patient management.

Potential Breakthroughs: Clinical trials create an environment for pharmaceutical companies and researchers to develop innovative therapies. These foster continuous advancements in the overall quality of healthcare. They offer a pathway for new drugs and treatments to reach the market and benefit patients with previously untreatable conditions.

Researchers are not always lucky to obtain the outcomes they predict, but the trial results still help scientists move in the correct direction.

Participants get access to promising new treatments that are not available outside the clinical trial boundaries. They also get the chance to be the first to benefit from a new method under study, to play an active role in their health care, and to clearly understand their disease or condition.

They are closely monitored, advised, cared for, and supported by a research team of doctors and other healthcare professionals.

They get the opportunity to help society by contributing to medical research.

Even if the participants do not directly benefit from the clinical trial, the information gained and gathered adds to the scientific knowledge and may be helpful for others.

Clinical trials can be a valuable treatment alternative, especially for patients with advanced or hard-to-treat diseases like cancer that have not responded to previous or current treatments.

Here are some examples of fruitful clinical trials: Immunotherapy for Cancer: Checkpoint inhibitors, such as pembrolizumab (Keytruda) and nivolumab (Opdivo), have shown remarkable success in treating various types of cancer, including melanoma, lung cancer, and bladder cancer.

Hepatitis C Treatment: Direct-acting antiviral drugs (DAAs) like sofosbuvir (Sovaldi) and ledipasvir/sofosbuvir (Harvoni) have demonstrated cure rates exceeding 95%, with minimal side effects, marking a significant improvement over older treatment regimens.

Gene Therapies: For spinal muscular atrophy (SMA) using gene therapy like Zolgensma have resulted in life-changing improvements for infants with this condition.

COVID-19 Vaccines: Pfizer-BioNTech, Moderna, and AstraZeneca vaccines have demonstrated high efficacy rates in preventing severe illness and death caused by the SARS-CoV-2 virus. These vaccines have been instrumental in curbing the global pandemic.

Targeted Therapies for Specific Mutations: Imatinib (Gleevec) for chronic myeloid leukaemia (CML) and trastuzumab (Herceptin) for HER2-positive breast cancer, have demonstrated impressive response rates by specifically targeting cancer cells harbouring particular genetic mutations.

Immunomodulatory Drugs for Autoimmune Diseases: Adalimumab (Humira) and infliximab (Remicade) have been transformative in managing autoimmune diseases like rheumatoid arthritis, psoriasis, and inflammatory bowel disease.

Deep Brain Stimulation (DBS) for Parkinson's Disease: Shown that it can effectively alleviate motor symptoms and improve the quality of life for individuals with Parkinson's disease who are unresponsive to medication.

CAR-T therapy for cancer: Chimeric Antigen Receptor T-cell Therapy (CAR-T) showed impressive results in treating certain types of leukaemia and lymphoma. CAR-T therapy involves modifying a patient's T cells to recognise and attack cancer cells effectively.

These are just a few examples of successful clinical trials that have had a profound impact on patient care and medical treatment. Clinical research continues to advance, and breakthroughs are continually being made to address various health conditions and improve outcomes for patients.

Demerits of clinical trials:
The new treatment may not be better than the standard treatment, as described below.

Adverse effects: A test drug may have side effects or risks that doctors don't know about or expect. This is especially true during phase I and phase II clinical trials.

The risk of side effects might be even greater for trials with cutting-edge approaches, such as gene therapy or new biological treatments. Some side effects may not have been fully identified during the trial period.

Generalizability: Some clinical trials have strict inclusion and exclusion criteria, making it challenging to generalise the results to a broader population, which could limit the applicability of the findings.

Bias and Confounding: In some cases, clinical trial results may be influenced by biases or confounding factors, leading to flawed conclusions that could impact patient care.

Duration of treatment: The clinical trial duration may be longer than the non-clinical trial treatments like hospital stays, more clinical trial site visits, etc.

Cost and Time: Clinical trials can be expensive and time-consuming endeavours. The lengthy process from initial research to regulatory approval can delay the availability of potentially beneficial treatments for patients.

Logistics: The trial site may not be available at a convenient location.

In summary, clinical trials can indeed be considered a double-edged sword, as they have both advantages and disadvantages. However, they play a vital role in shaping modern therapeutics by generating evidence-based data, optimising treatments, and establishing guidelines that help healthcare providers deliver the best possible care to patients. They are instrumental in bringing safe and effective treatments from the lab to clinical practise, ultimately improving patient outcomes and quality of life.

References:

1. Avicenna Journal of Medical Biotechnology [Internet]. [place unknown]: National Library of Medicine; 2016 [cited 2023 Jul 19]. Available from: https://www.ncbi.nlm.nih.gov/pmc/articles/PMC5124250/
2. National institute on aging [internet]. [place unknown]: National institute on aging; 2023 [cited 2023 Jul 19]. Available from: https://www.nia.nih.gov/health/what-are-clinical-trials-andstudies#:~:text=Clinical%20trials%20are%20research%20studies,safe%20and%20effective%20in%20people.
3. Clinical trials.gov [Internet]. [place unknown]: National Library of Medicine; [date unknown] [cited 2023 Jul 19]. Available from: https://clinicaltrials.gov/study-basics/learn-about-studies#ClinicalTrials
4. PhiSTAR [Internet]. India: PhiSTAR; 2022 [cited 2023 Jul 19]. Available from: https://www.phistar.in/why-clinical-trials-are-necessary-possible-advantages-and-disadvantages-of-clinical-trial/
5. Lawrence M. Friedman, Curt D. Furberg, David L. DeMets, David M. Reboussin, Christopher B. Granger. Fundamentals of Clinical Trials. 5th ed. Switzerland: Springer; 2015.

Chapter 21

Clinical Research Associate- A Prominent Role in Clinical Research

Mr. Dara Sai Ravi Teja, Pharm.D
Techsol Lifesciences, Madhapur, Hyderabad

Abstract
The main objective of this study is to elucidate the responsibilities of a Clinical Research Associate and the activities they perform during the entire trial in a detailed manner. This article is to spread awareness of the importance of clinical research associates and the activities they perform to ensure the smooth conduct of the trial in a detailed manner among researchers and healthcare professionals. CRA plays a prominent role in the entire clinical process, starting from the pre-site selection to the end of the study. All these aspects are discussed in detail in this article.

Objective:

The main objective of this study is to elucidate the responsibilities of a Clinical Research Associate and the activities they perform during the entire trial in a detailed manner.

Importance of the topic:

This article is to spread awareness of the importance of clinical research associates and the activities they perform to ensure the smooth conduct of the trial in a detailed manner among researchers and healthcare professionals.

Role in Clinical Trials:

CRA plays a prominent role in the entire clinical process, starting from the pre-site selection to the end of the study.

Pre-Site Selection: After getting the details regarding the clinical trial proposal from the sponsor, the CRA initiates the process of a pre-site visit by gathering information from investigators concerned with that particular department from different sites, either from CTRI or through some internal connections.

The CRA will contact the investigators and provide basic information about the study, such as indication, targeted population, etc., either by telephone or by email. Upon meeting the desired criteria, the CRA will provide a non-disclosure Agreement or confidentiality disclosure agreement to the investigator. A summary and feasibility questionnaire will be provided by the CRA upon signing the agreement with the investigator.

Site Selection:

Upon completion of the site feasibility questionnaire by the investigator and approval from the sponsor, CRA will conduct a site selection visit (SSV) either

Corresponding author: **Mr. Dara Sai Ravi Teja.** Can be contacted at phone number+91 9154370118 .
Email id: ravisai108@gmail

onsite or remotely upon the investigator's approval. CRA collects all the information regarding the facilities and previous trial experience and prepares a detailed report for the approval of the sponsor, protocol, and trial-related documents.

Site Initiation:

A clinical trial agreement will be signed by the investigator upon mutual approval from the sponsor on final and trial-related aspects. The investigator submits the EC dossier to the concerned ethics committee, and upon their approval, the trial is initiated. The CRA contacts the investigator to allocate dates for visiting the site and provides the SIV confirmation Letter along with the agenda upon acceptance from the investigator. During the SIV, CRA provides training on the protocol, Consent procedures, Safety information, SAE reporting, IP or Device details, etc. to the investigator and site staff. Subject recruitment is initiated upon acceptance from EC and providing all the trial-related documents to the site. The CRA provides an SIV Report to the sponsor along with action items, and upon their approval, a follow-up letter will be provided to the investigator.

Site Monitoring: During the trial period, CRA performs regular monitoring visits to ensure the smooth conduct of the trial. During Monitoring visits, the CRA reviews the documents and verifies the following activities:
- IP Accountability
- Protocol Deviations and EC Notifications
- Serious Adverse Events , adverse events at the site, and their appropriate reporting.
- Investigator Site File
- Informed Consent Documents
- Source Data Verification and Source Data Review

The CRA provides a detailed report on the trial activity to the sponsor, and upon their approval, a follow-up letter will be provided to the site.

Site Close-out:

Upon completion of the LPLV (Last Patient Last Visit) and collecting all the patient-related data, the CRA performs a site-close-out visit upon approval from the sponsor and investigator. All the trial-related documents, Action items, and IP/Device details should be carefully reviewed so that all site-related activities are completed and closed. A proper storage facility should be allocated to all trial-related documents for their archival as per the sponsor timelines. The investigator should notify the ethics committee regarding the completion of the trial, and a copy of it should be provided to the sponsor.

Limitations:

The major limitations the CRA experiences during their activities include improper communication from the site team, documentation errors, poor recruitment, Non-compliance with protocol, etc.

To tackle these limitations, the CRO organisation must implement efficient site management strategies by providing proper project management strategies. They include providing an efficient project management plan, regular monitoring visits to review the trial process, interim data analysis, and Regular communication with the site team.

Role of Technology:

Technology plays a crucial role in the overall impact of the trial process, with advancements in technology and the development of new tools and databases such as Medidata, Oracle, Octalsoft, etc.

These databases help monitor the regular progress of the trial. Data generated in the trial can be efficiently analysed using the technology. All the documentation errors can be communicated to the site team, and all issues can be resolved by generating appropriate queries and providing a mechanism to resolve them.

Conclusion:

Overall, A CRA acts as a liaison between the sponsor and site staff for the smooth conduct of the trial by providing proper monitoring, and oversight and ensuring protocol compliance at the site level. The involvement of CRA ensures validity, reliability, and advancement in health care.

References:

1. James R. Wright , ACS Journals, Factors that influence the recruitment of patients to Phase III studies in oncology-The perspective of the clinical research associate, https://doi.org/10.1002/cncr.10864. (Accessed 15 July 2023.)
2. Keun-Hee KIM , Journal of Korean Society for Clinical Pharmacology and Therapeutics ,The Study of Education and Qualification for the Maintenance of Clinical Research Associate (CRA) Professionalism, https://pesquisa.bvsalud.org/portal/resource/pt/wpr-206108. (Accessed 15 July 2023.)
3. Analysis and Assessment of Risk Management by the Clinical Research Associate, Base of Knowledge Warsaw University of Technology, https://repo.pw.edu.pl/info/master/WUT0f1eda53d57b413fa09d2fca5d3040f6/. (Accessed 15 July 2023.)

Chapter 22

Challenges Faced in Conducting Clinical Trials in Respiratory Medicine

Dr Puneet K Nagendra, MBBS, MD (Respiratory Medicine)
Assistant Professor, Department of Respiratoy Medicine
Dr Chandramma Dayananda Sagar Institute of Medical Education
and Research (A unit of Dayananda Sagar University)
Devarakaggalahalli, Harohalli Hobali, Kanakapura Taluk, Ramanagara District, Karnataka

Abstract

To increase the effectiveness and validity of clinical trials in respiratory medicine, this article examines some of the major difficulties encountered during the procedure and suggests certain logical remedies. We discuss these issues in the context of the recruitment and retention of patients, the varied patient population, the placebo response and binding, compliance and adherence, safety, and ethical issues related to conducting clinical trials fairly in the field of respiratory medicine.

INTRODUCTION:

The treatment of several lung disorders and diseases, which impact on a sizeable population globally, is greatly influenced by the advances in Respiratory Medicine. In this area, clinical trials are crucial for furthering medical understanding, creating novel medicines, and enhancing patient outcomes. Researchers and healthcare workers must overcome several obstacles when conducting clinical trials in respiratory medicine. We brainstorm by addressing some of the major difficulties encountered when carrying out clinical trials in respiratory medicine and provide possible methods to improve the effectiveness and validity of such trials.

Patient Recruitment and Retention:

"The incidence of patient availability sharply decreases when a clinical trial begins and returns to its original level as soon as the trial is completed."
Lasagna's Law (1970)

Ensuring the right number of qualified patients are recruited and kept on board during clinical trials in respiratory medicine is one of the biggest problems. Since many respiratory disorders are very uncommon, it can be difficult to obtain a large enough pool of participants. Additionally, due to their health issues or other logistical limitations, people with severe respiratory diseases may be unable or unwilling to participate in lengthy trials that are physically and mentally taxing.

Corresponding author: Dr Puneeth K Nagendra. Can be contacted at phone number+91 99454 55774 .
Email id: drpuneet.kn@gmail

Collaboration across several hospitals, clinics, and research facilities can help to increase patient recruitment efforts and grow the patient pool. Improved patient retention may also result from the design of patient-centered trials, payment for participation, and use of telemedicine techniques for remote monitoring can bring in more patients and help to retain them in the study. [1]

Heterogeneous Patient Population:

Respiratory disorders encompass a wide range of conditions, each with their unique characteristics and manifestations. It may be challenging to identify the homogeneous subgroups for analysis due to the patient population's heterogeneity, which might make it difficult to interpret the trial results appropriately.

The study population's homogeneity can be increased by prioritizing stratified recruitment depending on the disease's severity, subtype, or pertinent biomarkers. It may also be possible to find subgroups that respond better to therapies by utilizing personalized medicine strategies and including genetic data into the trial design are the potential solutions for this. [2]

Compliance and Adherence:

Ensuring patient compliance and adherence to the treatment regimen is essential for respiratory medicine trials for obtaining valid results. However, symptoms brought on by respiratory disorders like asthma and chronic obstructive pulmonary disease (COPD) may lead to non-adherence or premature dropout.

Reminders sent to patients and electronic monitoring devices are two solutions that can aid with adherence rates. Additionally, educating patients thoroughly and clearly about the value of compliance and addressing potential adverse effects can have a favorable effect on their behavior.

Placebo Response and Blinding:

Placebo response, a phenomenon whereby patients in the control group experience better because of psychological or other causes, can dramatically affect the results of respiratory medicine trials. Blinding is intended to mitigate this effect , but it can be difficult to implement, especially in trials including therapies like inhalers or other devices with observable effects.

Simple solutions like adopting double-blind placebo-controlled designs or a robust blinding strategy can reduce the placebo response and improve the validity of trial outcomes. [4]

Safety and ethical concerns:

Participants in clinical trials may face dangers, thus it is crucial to ensure their safety. Trials for respiratory treatment must carefully evaluate potential adverse effects because participants may already have impaired lung function.

To address the safety issues and sustain ethical standards, comprehensive and stringent safety protocols, informed consent procedures, and frequent participant monitoring might be helpful.

CONCLUSION:

Clinical trials must be conducted in respiratory medicine to advance scientific understanding and enhance patient care. Despite the issues raised, innovative approaches, collaboration, and technological advancements offer promising solutions. Researchers can advance respiratory research by addressing these challenges and continue to make strides in respiratory medicine, leading to better treatment options and improved outcomes for patients suffering with respiratory illness.

REFERENCES:

1. Chaudhari N, Ravi R, Gogtay NJ, Thatte UM. Recruitment and retention of the participants in clinical trials: Challenges and solutions. Perspect Clin Res. 2020 Apr-Jun;11(2):64-69.

2. Sonu Subudhi et al. Strategies to minimize heterogeneity and optimize clinical trials in Acute Respiratory Distress (ARDS): Insights from mathematical modelling. eBioMedicine 2022;75: 103809

3. Mingkun Yu, Ziyi Lin, Changhao Liang et al. How to improve participant compliance and retention in clinical trials: A Scoping Review, 20 November 2020.

4. Haflidadóttir SH, Juhl CB, Nielsen SM, Henriksen M, Harris IA, Bliddal H, Christensen R. Placebo response and effect in randomized clinical trials: meta-research with focus on contextual effects. Trials. 2021 Jul 26;22(1):493.

5. Robert A. Wise. Ethical Issues Confronted in Pulmonary Clinical Trials. Proc Am Thorac Soc Vol 4. pp 200–205, 2007.

Brochure of
MPS National Clinical
Trial Summit—2023

MPS NATIONAL CLINICAL TRIAL SUMMIT—2023

AUG 5-6, 2023, 4.00 PM TO 8.00 PM(ONLINE CONFERENCE)

(Since 2016)

Main Sponsor	Associate Sponsor	In association with Dept. of Pharmacology	In association with JPADR Journal
Clini Med LIFESCIENCES PRIVATE LIMITED	ETHIXINN Your Research Companion	 CDSIMER Dr. Chandramma Dayananda Sagar Institute of Medical Education and Research	JPADR

Organizing Chairman	Organizing Secretary	Moderators		Organizing team	
		Day one	Day two		

Dr. Basavanna PL	Dr. Shiva Murthy N	Dr. Chinmaya Mahapatra	Dr. Sanjeev Gupta	Mr. Dara Sai Ravi Teja	Dr. Siva Sankar Parasa

Prestigious Panel of Speakers

Dr. Shambo S Samajdar	Dr. Somanath Basu	Dr. Suyog Sindhu	Mr. Anirudh Sahoo	Dr. Gayathri Vishwakarma

Dr. Sapna Patil	Mrs. Vaishali Deshpande	Dr. Anuradha HV	Mr. Snehendu Koner

Dr. Meeta Amit Burande	Mrs. Renuka Neogi	Dr. Prajakt Barde	Dr. Akash Gadgade

Dr. Abhijit Munshi	Mrs. Lakshmi Achuta	Ms. Karishma Rampilla	Mr. Manish Singh Yadav

Program—Day 1

Topics	Speakers
Welcome address	**Dr. Shiva Murthy N, MBBS, MD, MBA.,** President MPS, and Associate Professor, Dept of Pharmacology, CDSIMER, Ramanagara, Karnataka.
Inaugural key note speech	**Dr. Basavanna PL, MBBS, MD.,** Board member, MPS, and HOD, Dept of Clinical Pharmacology, MMCRI, Mysuru, Karnataka.
Moderator of the day—Instructions to participants and introduction of speakers	**Dr. Chinmaya Mahapatra, PhD.,** Assoc. Professor & HOD, TNU //LQPPV (PvOI) IntuVigilance, UK.// Editor-in-Chief, JPADR Journal //Founder President Global Pharmacovigilance Society. Odisha.
New Drug Clinical Trial Rule-2019—A brief update	**Dr. Somanath Basu PhD, Scientist E, QMS and Regulatory affairs, AMTZ,** Vishakhapatnam, Andrapradesh Ex-Deputy Drug Controller (I), CDSCO, MOHFW, Govt of India.
Evolution of GCP and Principles of GCP	**Dr. Chinmaya Mahapatra and Dr. Shiva Murthy N..** (see details above)
Indian and international regulations governing clinical research	**Dr Shambo S Samajdar MBBS MD DM,** PG Dip Endo & Diab (RCP, UK), Dip Allergy Asthma Immunology (AAAAI), Fellowship Respiratory & Critical Care (WBUHS), Clinical Pharmacologist, School of Tropical Medicine & Consultant, Diabetes & Allergy-Asthma Therapeutics Specialty Clinic Kolkata, West Bengal.
Protocol components and Clinical trial designing	**Dr Suyog Sindhu MBBS MD, FAIMER (2020), MFILIPE,** Associate Professor, Department of Pharmacology and Therapeutics, King George's Medical University, Lucknow, Uttar Pradesh
Documents required for regulatory submission and the current procedure for CT application approval in India	**Mr. Anirudh Sahoo. M. Pharm,** Senior Project Manager, George Clinical, Bengaluru, Karnataka.
Sample size, Data capturing, CRFs development, Randomization, Blinding/Concealment, and CDM tools	**Dr Gayathri Vishwakarma MSc, PhD (Statistics), MBA (Quality Management),** Lead Biostatistician, George Institute for Global Health, New Delhi.
Principles of ethics in clinical research and Ethics committee composition	**Dr Sapna Patil MBBS MD** PGDMLE, CCEBDM, PDCR,PCPV and GCP, PGDMLE from National Law School, Bangalore, CCEBDM from PHFI, Associate Professor, Department of Pharmacology, Sapthagiri institute of medical sciences and research center, Bengaluru , Karnataka.
Ethics committee Responsibilities, Functioning, Approvals and Records management	**Mrs Vaishali Deshpande Chairperson, Ethics committee,** Ruby hall clinic, Sancheti Hospital, Joshi Hospital, Pune, Maharashtra, Ex research officer at Diabetes unit, KEM Hospital research centre, Mumbai., Maharash-
Patients responsibilities, Patient selection, Randomization and its concerns from patient point of view	**Ms. Renuka Neogi B. Pharm, MSc (CR, ICRI),** PGD Pharmaceutical Management (ICRI), DBM, RQAP-GCP (Society of Quality assurance), CCRA (ACRP), Deputy General Manager & Head – Global Clinical Quality Management, Global Clinical Development, Sun Pharmaceutical Industries Limited. Mumbai, Maharashtra.

End of the day 1 Proceedings

Program—Day 2

Topics	Speakers
Welcome address	**Dr. Shiva Murthy N, MBBS, MD, MBA.,** President MPS, and Associate Professor, Dept of Pharmacology, CDSIMER, Ramanagara, Karnataka.
Moderator of the day—Instructions to participants and introduction of speakers	**Dr. Sanjeev Gupta MBBS (MD Moscow), MD Pharmacology,** Associate Professor, Dept of Pharmacology, Govt Medical College, Kathua, J & K.
Responsibilities of Investigators	**Dr. Anuradha HV, MBBS, MD.,** Professor and HOD, Dept of Pharmacology, MS Ramaiah Medical College, Bengaluru, Karnataka.
Responsibilities of Site Management Organization (SMO)	**Mr. Snehendu Koner, MA (American Lit, Stanley Ind, USA),** Head, Business Development, CliniMed LifeSciences, Regional Coordinator, India , Avoidable Deaths Network (ADN) , Kolkata, West Bengal.
Contents of Informed consent document and consenting procedures (methodology)	**Dr. Meeta Amit Burande MBBS, MD Pharmacology,** Professor, Dept of Pharmacology, D Y Patil Medical College, Kolhapur, Maharashtra.
Sponsor responsibilities	**Dr. Prajakt Barde MBBS, MD (Seth GSMC and KEM hospital),** Founder and Director of Med Indite Communications Pvt Ltd, Executive Medical Director, AUM Biosciences, Mumbai, Maharashtra.
Definitions and importance of ADRs reporting, Pharamcovigilance, ICSR, PSUR, DSUR, PBRER etc, ADRs, SAEs, CT Safety reporting requirements/ Timelines.	**Dr. Akash Gadgade MBBS, MD Pharmacology,** Associate Director Medical & Scientific Affairs at Navitas Life Sciences, Belgaum, Karnataka
Review of safety documents by regulators/ ethics committees and compensation for SAEs/Deaths as per Indian gazette notifications/ clinical trial rules.	**Dr. Abhijit Munshi B.A.M.S. M.D. (in Alternative Medicine),** P.G. Diploma In Clinical Research, M.A. in Sanskrit, MBA Healthcare Administration, Director –Clinical Operations & Academics, Alchemy Clinical Research Services, and Ethics Committee Trainer / Consultant. Nagpur, Maharashtra.
Investigational product management	**Mrs. Lakshmi Achuta Master of Science (M.Sc.), Applied Botany, MS Quality Management (BITS Pilani),** Strategic Advisor - Biotech, Pharmaceuticals & Medical Devices, Bengaluru, Karnataka
Clinical trial Quality management, remote monitoring and Site based auditing.	**Ms. Karishma Rampilla B.tech, M.tech, (Biotechnology),** PGD clinical research, Director & Founder Cavaxion Clinical Research Pvt Ltd., Hyderabad, Telangana.
Fraud and Misconduct in clinical research and its consequences	**Mr. Manish Singh Yadav, MS** (Analytical Instrumentation and Chemical analysis), **(PhD Bio-analytical Chemistry Pursuing),** Founder and CEO of Ethixinn CRS, Madhya Pradesh
Vote of thanks and Closing note	**Dr. Basavanna PL** Organizing Chairman and **Dr. Shiva Murthy N** Organizing Secretary

End of the conference, Collection of feedback. E-Certificate distribution—within 1.5 week

MPS NATIONAL CLINICAL TRIAL SUMMIT—2023
AUG 5-6, 2023, 4.00 PM TO 8.00 PM
(ONLINE CONFERENCE)

(Since 2016)

Targeted Audience

Industry Participants
- Professionals and consultants working in Pharma industry, CRO Industry, SMOs, KPOs etc.
- Professionals working for development of pharmaceuticals, neutraceuticals, biologicals, alternative medicines (AYUSH) etc.
- Sponsors of CTs, Senior management and directors working in above industries
- Ethics committee members
- Hospital Doctors and their team members who are working in clinical trials as investigators
- Anyone who is interested to make career in clinical research industry

Academics Participants
Students of
- Graduate and Postgraduate students, Medical, Dental, Paramedical sciences
- B Pharma, M Pharma, Pharma D, B.Tech (Biotech), Msc Pharmacology, MSc Clinical Research, PGD in clinical research, regulatory affairs, Quality assurance, Biology, Chemistry etc
- Teaching faculty—Junior/Senior faculty
- Ethics committee members
- BAMS/BUMS/BHMS students and other alternative medicine students who are interested to make career in clinical research industry

Registration Support team (WhatsApp No.)

Mr. D S Ravi Teja
+91 91543 70118

Dr. Siva Sankar P
+91 91103 37908

Dr Shiva Murthy N
+91 88843 28275

Dr Sanjeev Gupta
+91 94197 63076

Email ID for queries:
mps.mdpharmacologists@gmail.com

Note: Confirmation mail sent by us may sit in spam folder. Please check once before contacting us.

Registration Fee

Type of Participant	Early bird registration (till 20th July, 2023)	Till 31st July, 2023	1st August to 04th August, 2023 (No Spot registration)
Students	Rs. 400	Rs. 500	Rs. 600
Academicians	Rs. 500	Rs. 600	Rs. 700
Industry Professionals and Consultants	Rs. 600	Rs. 700	Rs. 800

How to Register (Use link)
(All registered participants will get e-Certificate of participation)

→

Click to get registration link
https://forms.gle/eu4nggLPT6w2Z1zKA

Bank Account Details for Registration

Account details for making payments:

Acc. Name: Medical Pharmacologist Society

Acc. No: 185001000497,

Bank: ICICI Bank

Branch: Kothanur, Bangalore,

IFSC code: ICIC0001850

Or

Scan the QR code given in

→

MPS NATIONAL CLINICAL TRIAL SUMMIT—2023
AUG 5-6, 2023, 4.00 PM TO 8.00 PM
(ONLINE CONFERENCE)
(Since 2016))

About Medical Pharmacologists Society
(MPS = MD Pharmacologists. Let us Unite, Innovate, Serve)

- MPS is a registered society as per Karnataka Society Registration Act, (1960). It is a not for profit organization. This prestigious society conducted many programs successfully since 2016.
- MPS society made efforts to serve the profession by providing opportunities to learn cutting edge techniques related to pharmacogenomics, flow cytometry, GCP, clinical trial methodology, career guidance, etc. More details about the society can be found in society's website—Click to visit the website (https://mpsmdpharmac.org/)
- Life membership: All MD Pharmacologists are eligible to become life members. Through this event, we request everyone to support and strengthen the society by becoming life members and participating in our events. Click the link to join as life member of MPS (https://mpsmdpharmac.org/membership/)

About CliniMed Life Sciences Pvt Ltd

CliniMed LifeSciences is a Contract Research Organization focused on improvement of patient care globally using data, technology, modern analytics, and innovation in therapeutics. The company has been founded with the objective to accelerate the process of clinical research for the clients in the field of both new drugs and medical devices. CliniMed's team is specialized on clinical development, early phase development, regulatory affairs, and medical experts in a broad range of therapeutic indications. Support the customers in their clinical development planning and implementation. CliniMed, strives to ensure costs are kept within the budget using n-depth knowledge of international and local regulatory requirements and network of global investigators to ensure that the trial objectives are met on time. Click the link to visit the company website (https://www.clinimedlifesciences.com/)

About Ethixinn CRS

Established in 2014, Ethixinn CRS is a Pharmaceutical and Environmental Research Solution Provider. Ethixinn CRS has been designed to provide a broad range of Scientific, Quality and Regulatory Services for Pharma/ Biopharma Research, Environmental Research, Collaborative Research and QAT [Quality (GxP) Accreditations & Trainings] globally. Ethixinn CRS along with its strong pool of research collaborators is a perfect blend of expertise, technology and innovative ideas to provide reliable, cost-effective, technology driven services and practically implementable solutions to the clients/partners. Ethixinn CRS's commitment to ethics, quality and customer-focused approach bundled with outstanding expertise distinguishes them from others. To know more about the company click the link (https://ethixinn.com/).

About CDSIMER

Dr.Chandramma Dayananda Sagar Institute of Medical Education and Research (CDSIMER) has been established under the aegis of Dayananda Sagar University (DSU), a proud member of the Dayananda Sagar Institutions (DSI) family. Spread over 140 acres, DSU campus is located in Harohalli in greater Bengaluru area. CDSIMER offers comprehensive facilities for teaching, research and patient-care. The Institute will be attached to a state-of-the-art 1350 bed hospital facility equipped with modern medical infrastructure that will allow to train future ready doctors. These young doctors will be tuned to become one of the finest professionals in the world, with a passion to serve humanity, especially the sick and needy. More details about CDSIMER is available at **https://cdsimer.edu.in/ (click the link to visit CDSIMER website)**

About JPADR

The Journal of Pharmacovigilance and Drug Research (JPADR) is the official publication of the Global Pharmacovigilance Society. This is an international, open access, and peer-reviewed scientific journal. It focuses on pharmacovigilance studies and their associated topics such as adverse drug reaction, drug clinical trials, drug effectiveness and efficacy, drugs risk management, as well as all aspects related to the safe use of drugs.
Abstracting and Indexing: National Digital Library of India, Google Scholar, Geneva foundation for medical education and research, J-Gate, ResearchBib, EuroPub, Zenodo, OpenAIRE etc. Visit journal website by clicking the link (https://jpadr.com/index.php/jpadr) to know the scope and other details about the journal.

Medical Pharmacologists Society

Edition—01

© Copyrights 2023

Clinical Trial Management

"Developed by Clinical Research Professionals; For Clinical Researchers"
A collaborative effort by organizers, speakers and participants of the MPS NCTS 2023 conference

Dr Shiva Murthy N MBBS, MD, MBA.,
Founder president, MPS and Asso. Professor, Department of Pharmacology, CDSIMER.

- 22+ yrs Post MD experience (13 yrs industry and 09 yrs medical college),
- Managing Editor, JPADR journal, Reviewer, IJP Journal, First rank in MD pharmacology 2001, RGUHS. Awarded 1st prize (2021) and 2nd prize (2022) for pharmacovigilance related short movies during NPW celebration, Issued by NCC-IPC under PVPI, Govt of India, Awarded 2nd prize (2021) for oral scientific paper presentation at Hyperpiesia conference held at Chennai, His projects received Research Society Merit Certificate (2003) at St John's medical college, and 3rd prize for the oral presentation (2003) at SRC-IPS Conference, He was Awarded "INSC Research Excellence Award - 2023" for his work on NSAIDs and SARs.
- Published an e-Book titled "Pharmacovigilance Reflective Writing E-Book" (this book featured in Uppsala reports (an official publication of UMC, WHO), 16 publications in peer reviewed journals,15 presentations (national & international conferences)

Dr Basavanna P L MBBS, MD.
Professor and Head, Clinical Pharmacology Mysure Medical College and Research Center. (MMCRI, Mysuru)

- Board member, MPS
- Nodal officer—Ayushman Digital Mission
- Vice President, PAGE (Peoples Association for Geriatric Empowerment, Mysure
- State Nodal Officer, Materiovigilance Programme of India
- Nodal Officer, Digital Mission Mode Project—I and II, MCI, New Delhi
- Coordinator, Pharmacovigilance Center, MMCRI.
- Authored More than 30 scientific articles in peer reviewed journals.
- Member, MEU, Assessor MCI, Examiner—UG/PG RGUHS/Other universities, Member of BOS, RGUHS.
- Vice President, MMCRI Teachers Association.

Dr. Chinmaya Mahapatra, M Pharma, PhD
Founder of Global Pharmacovigilance Society, Editor –in-Chief of JPADR journal, Assoc. Prof and HOD of Pharmaceutics.

- Gold Medal Awardee in Masters degree, PhD with DST INSPIRED Fellowship.
- 10+ yrs experience in pharmacovigilance and pharamaceuticals field. Industry experience as QA.
- Working as LQPPV (PVOI) for intuvigilance,
- Published a book titled "Fundamental concepts of Pharmacy and its Application", Published 9 scientific articles in peer reviewed journals.
- Patents—four Indian patents, 2 German patents to his credit.
- Certified member of Association of clinical research professionals (ACRP)

Dr Sanjeev Gupta MD Moscow (MBBS), MD Pharmacology (India),
Diabetes-AGC (University of Copenhagen)

- Associate Professor, Dept of Pharmacology, Govt. Medical College, Kathua,
- Editorial Board Member, JPADR
- Ex-Deputy coordinator, Pharmacovigilance center (AMC) ASCOMS &H, Jammu
- 12 publications in indexed journals
- Presented papers in National and International Conferences
- Worked as curriculum committee member at GMC & AH, Rajouri, Jammu and Kashmir.

Address for communication/Office address:
Dr Shiva Murthy N, SowmyaShiva Sadana, No 57, 1st cross, 4th main, Kothanur Dinne, JP Nagar 8th Phase, Bangalore – 560078, Karnataka, India
Phone: +91 8884328275
Email: mps.mdpharmacologists@gmail.com
We do not have any other office.
For sales, please write to mps.mdpharmacologists@gmail.com

Cost: Price: Hard bound copy—10 USD (Ten USD only)

9798861512572

Printed in Great Britain
by Amazon